A
BRAND
FROM
THE
BURNING

by *Alcyon Ruth Fleck*

A true story of the life of a Roman Catholic priest and of his conversion to the Seventh-day Adventist Church, where he is now a minister.

TEACH Services, Inc.
Brushton, New York

Facsimile Reproduction

As this book played a formative role in the development of Christian thought
and the publisher feels that this book, with its candor and depth, still holds
significance for the church today. Therefore the publisher has chosen to
reproduce this historical classic from an original copy. Frequent variations in the
quality of the print are unavoidable due to the condition of the original.
Thus the print may look darker or lighter or appear to be missing detail, more
in some places than in others.

2006   07   08   09   10   11   12   ·   5   4   3   2   1

Copyright © 1960 Pacific Press Publising Association
Copyright © 2006 TEACH Services, Inc.
ISBN-13: 978-1-57258-445-7
ISBN 1-57258-445-9
Library of Congress Control Number: 2006927617

Published by

TEACH Services, Inc.
www.TEACHServices.com

PREFACE

This fascinating biography, telling of the search for truth by a Roman Catholic priest, is authentic in all details. The names of the principal characters have been changed for obvious reasons. Today Andrés is a successful minister, carrying on soul-winning endeavor in the Seventh-day Adventist Church.

The author is personally acquainted with many of the experiences related in this volume. The facts have been checked carefully to make certain the story is authentic.

There is no more thrilling search in life than to go forward in a spiritual quest, seeking God's answer to the unsolved problems of the soul. It is a courageous act when a man or woman breaks with the traditions and customs of his family because of his sincere faith in what he believes to be true. This is a spiritual saga that should be an inspiration to every Christian who stands firm in his religious convictions.

—**The Publishers.**

DEDICATION

In the preparation of this story I am, first of all, indebted to Andrés himself. Without reservation, he co-operated in every way in giving all necessary information. When approached about the prospect of his story being printed, he replied, "If the telling of my experience can help someone else to find this wonderful truth, then, of course, I give my consent wholeheartedly."

Watching the transformation of heart and mind of this child of God has been one of our most thrilling personal experiences in soul winning. We pray that God will continue to give Andrés the victory in the future as He did in the greatest conflict of his life when "the human intelligence had to humble itself before the divine word."

Help and encouragement has been given me by my husband, Kenneth. His life, devoted unstintingly to being a "fisher of men," is a constant inspiration to me. To him I lovingly dedicate *A Brand From the Burning*.

—The Author.

CONTENTS

1

THE SONS OF MARIA

"**C**LOP, clop, clop," came the sound of the horse's hoofs down the quiet village street one bright spring afternoon. Aunt Marta was returning from the neighboring small town, where she had gone to market. With her on the horse she carried a five-gallon can of milk and her large egg basket with about ten dozen eggs.

Aunt Marta, a heavy-set jolly woman, could be heard singing as she neared the home of her sister. María and her two sons, Andrés and José, aged nine and eleven respectively, lived with María's parents in a quaint village in the mountains of northern Spain.

The two boys had been practicing their archery, a popular sport among the boys of this rural community. José had placed an old hat on a stump in the yard. From the inside of the house, through an open door, the boys took turns shooting their arrows at the target.

"Oh, Andrés, I hear Aunt Marta returning from the market," exclaimed José.

"Let's go to meet her," answered Andrés; "but first, I am going to hit that hat once more."

At that moment Aunt Marta rounded the corner of the house and entered the yard. So well-timed was Andrés's shot, that the arrow, instead of hitting the hat, sank into a hind leg of his aunt's horse.

How so much could take place in such a short time is a mystery. The frightened horse, disregarding his passenger and her precious load of milk and eggs, gave one series of jumps and kicks in an effort to rid himself of the painful barb in his leg. Poor Aunt Marta, totally unprepared for the horse's antics, soon found herself in a ditch filled with mud from the spring thaw, the milk and eggs mixed up like an eggnog on top of her.

The boys' mother, hearing the commotion, came running from the kitchen. She had just put the last of twenty loaves of bread into her large Dutch oven, after removing the hot coals.

"What can be happening!" María thought as she gathered her skirts about her and ran in the direction of the shrieks and pounding horse's hoofs.

"Aunt Marta, what has happened?" she asked as she helped the woman emerge from the muddy mess.

"Those two boys must know something about this," Aunt Marta said, recovering herself.

"José, go and call your brother. I think there is some straightening out to be done here," María charged the older boy.

Young Andrés came out of hiding with fear and trembling. Having had previous experience with the firm discipline of his mother, he knew that punishment was certain.

He approached his mother, guilt written all over his face. "Did you call me, mamma?"

"Andrés, did you hit Aunt Marta's horse with an arrow?"

"Yes, mamma, I did, but I didn't mean to. I was trying

to hit the hat," Andrés attempted desperately to explain.

"That may be true, my son, but you must learn caution when playing with bow and arrows. More than that, you were a coward and ran away."

The punishment that María administered was not soon forgotten. With her husband in faraway Argentina, María often found the burden of managing the home, the farm, and her boys a heavy one. Her parents were able to help, although grandma was not as spry as she once was. She helped with the housework and training of the boys. During the planting and harvesting seasons, the responsibility of guiding the old, hand-hewn plow behind the oxen, sowing the grain, and planting the potatoes, garbanzos, lentils, beans, and other vegetables fell on María's slight shoulders.

Her father, unable to do heavy work, cared for the family's flock of sheep. In the winter months, when the mountains were covered with snow, he took the sheep to lower altitudes where green grass could be found.

For the hardy people of this rural village in the rugged highlands of the province of León, life was hard. They subsisted entirely on the products of their land. Living as they did, where many of the mountains seemed to be solid rock, their homes were built sturdily of stones, cemented together with clay. Because of the severe winters, when the doors were often blocked shut during a snowstorm, it was the custom to build two-story houses. The ground floor was used as a barn for the storage of grain, hay, and corn, and as a shelter for the animals.

The upper story served as the living quarters for the

family. María's home had a spacious kitchen, with a home-made stove constructed of stones lined with cement. The baking was done in the huge Dutch oven built into the wall. The furniture was hand-carved, sturdily constructed. María's kitchen had a long table that served as the family board. Although money was scarce, food was abundant, as the result of María's thrift.

In addition to two other rooms that served as bedrooms, there was a small room set apart as a place of prayer. Despite the long and tedious hours spent in the fields, and the burden of being both father and mother to her children, María never neglected the religious life of her family. The rosaries and prayers were faithfully learned and repeated. Andrés and José were led to the prayer room and taught to kneel and say their prayers to the various saints whose images and pictures were found on the walls. The candles were lighted at the home altar, and during the summer flowers were placed there. Everything was done to provide a religious atmosphere for the children.

When other duties took María from home, the grandmother took her place as religious instructor. Among the teachings that remained in Andrés's mind was the grandmother's emphasis on the doctrine that individual judgment took place at death.

"After a person dies," she said, "the soul goes to meet God, but Satan deters him in the road and asks, 'My friend, where are you going?' The good soul replies, 'Friend of yours, no; servant of God, yes. I have always kept the commandments of God. Amen.' But Satan follows him, asking what the Ten Commandments are from the first to the last.

If the soul knows them, he is a friend of God. If not, the devil binds him with ten chains and carries him to hell."

From his early years, Andrés was filled with a fear of hell. He was constantly reminded of his moral obligations, and he longed to escape the torments that awaited the wicked. However, being a boy with mischievous ideas, he often fell into temptation.

One summer day young Andrés found time heavy on his hands. Mother and José were away and grandmother had fallen asleep in her chair. The lazy atmosphere of the day, broken only by bird calls, noises of animals, and the monotonous droning of the bees, did not seem to satisfy the active mind of the boy. He searched for excitement.

Walking down the dusty road to the river, he swung a stick he had picked up along the road. Not stopping at the river, he crossed the rustic bridge and continued on up the slope on the other side.

Suddenly his attention was drawn to a prune orchard at one side of the road. He knew that the trees belonged to José Vásquez, an old farmer, who was often seen in one of the wine saloons of the town. Andrés's conscience didn't fail him. As his mouth watered for the juicy, ripe fruit that he saw on the loaded trees, he hesitated, remembering, "Thou shalt not steal."

"Old Don José will never miss a prune or two; there's not a soul in sight," he said to himself to quiet his disturbing thoughts.

In a flash he was over the fence and up the nearest tree. His jacket served as a container to carry the stolen fruit, and before long he had it well filled.

As the boy made ready to carry his cargo down the tree, he was startled to hear a shout. "Hey there! Get out of my tree!" It was old José himself.

Fear clutched at the throat of the boy and his heart beat a wild tempo as he half slid and half jumped to the ground. The angry farmer was rapidly approaching, intent on catching the culprit who dared to trespass on his property. Youth had the advantage, however, and Andrés cleared the fence and soon left the river and bridge in the distance in his mad dash for home and safety.

"Andrés! Whatever is the matter?" María exclaimed as her young son ran past her toward the bedroom.

María shut the door and turned to follow Andrés, but she turned back when she heard a loud knock on the door. While his mother went to the door, Andrés made his escape to a more secluded part of the house.

"That boy of yours!" the irate man fairly shouted. "He was stealing my prunes! See, is this not his jacket? He left it in the tree as he ran."

"I am so sorry, señor. Yes, it is Andrés's jacket. Please forgive him. He will be punished, never fear," María answered apologetically.

Having accomplished his purpose, the man left, and Andrés soon found himself face to face with a serious mother carrying the telltale jacket.

"Andrés," she spoke slowly.

"Yes, mamma," the repentant boy answered, eyes to the floor.

"Are you a thief, my son?" María turned his face up to hers as she questioned him.

"I don't know," he sobbed. "I promise that I'll never do it again."

To be sure that his repentance was sincere and that he would not forget the lesson, María led Andrés to the place where the rod was kept and gave him his punishment with her firm but kind hand.

2

BOYHOOD PRANKS

"JOSE! Call your brother to help us. This sack of wheat has to be cleaned before we can take the grain to the mill. Our flour supply is almost gone," María instructed her older son. "Where is Andrés?"

"I think he is playing marbles with Pedro down the street," answered José.

"You don't mean Pedro Martínez!" exclaimed his mother.

"Yes," answered José. "I saw them there on the street only a few minutes ago."

"I have told you boys again and again that Pedro is not fit company. He never goes to church; he spends his time getting into trouble on the street. Please bring Andrés here this minute." The woman spoke firmly.

María and her mother sat at the long table in the kitchen, cleaning the golden kernels of wheat that had been harvested from their fields. Today they would take a sack to the village mill, which was built over the clear, swift waters of the mountain stream.

"Do you want me?" Andrés asked as he entered the room.

"I certainly do want you, young man. Where have you been?" María asked.

"He was down the street playing with Pedro, all right,"

offered José, who, like most brothers and sisters, was glad to furnish information about his delinquent brother.

María sighed as she looked at her young son standing with his head hanging dejectedly. He had been well instructed as to whom his mother considered to be fit company. Some of the village boys who spent their time in mischief-making were not as carefully reared as were Andrés and José. María was anxious that her boys keep away from bad influences.

The mother decided that some punishment must be meted out. Knowing how well Andrés enjoyed going to the mill with her, she said, "For your disobedience, Andrés, you will have to stay here and finish cleaning the wheat. You are not to leave the house while we are gone."

Andrés's face clouded. Since morning he had been looking forward to the trip to the mill. He knew, however, that tears or coaxing would avail nothing. Past experience had taught him that when mother made a decision, there was no changing it.

When the rest of the family had gone and the rattle of the oxcart faded away, the house seemed strangely quiet. He was seldom in the house when both mother and grandmother were away.

"Well, I might just as well get started," he said to himself. "There really isn't much left to clean."

After the last of the grains of wheat had been dropped into the pan, Andrés began to wander from room to room, searching for something to occupy his time and to help him forget the oppressive silence. He sat on the steps leading to the yard, chin in his hand.

Suddenly there was a streak across the yard with Skip, his little dog, in fast pursuit. Skip seemed to find his greatest delight in chasing the neighbor's cat.

"I wonder why dogs and cats can't be friends," mused Andrés. A light came into his eyes and a smile spread across his face as a plan began to formulate in his mind, one that was sure to bring him nothing but trouble.

He quickly went to the room where the feed was kept and found a large grain sack. Next he caught his little dog. So far the plan was working smoothly, but gaining the confidence of the cat was more of a problem.

"Come, kitty, kitty," he coaxed.

Finally, with both cat and dog corraled, he first put the cat into the sack and then Skip.

There ensued the most bloodcurdling, weird yelps and howls as cat and dog prepared to fight to the death.

Once in the sack together, the damage was done. Altnough Andrés soon repented of his foolish idea, he saw that it was impossible to remedy the situation.

"Oh, dear! What shall I do?" Andrés thought desperately.

The cat's claws proved to be vicious weapons, and blood began to come through the sack as it writhed and rolled on the ground. Neighbors arrived, carrying clubs and sticks. At this point, Andrés saw no alternative but to put some distance between himself and the terrible commotion in front of his house.

Watching from his hiding place, Andrés trembled as he saw the alcalde, the mayor of the town, arrive. It was his job to maintain the peace.

In the midst of the fight, Andrés's mother and grandmother arrived in their cart. Seeing the crowd congregated in her yard, María was fearful that something had happened to Andrés.

"What has happened?" she asked one of the bystanders.

Then she saw the cause of the disturbance. Someone had managed to get hold of one corner of the sack, and Skip came trembling out. His muzzle was torn and bleeding. The owner of the cat rescued her animal and carried her home, making remarks about boys who were cruel to animals.

A grim look came over María's face as she began looking for Andrés.

"What will I ever do with that boy?" she thought.

When the last of the curious spectators had dispersed, Andrés ventured from his hiding place.

"There you are, Andrés. Why were you hiding?" his mother asked.

Andrés had nothing to say, but the guilty look on his face spoke eloquently. Later, he comforted himself with Skip in his arms. "I'm sorry, Skip. I didn't mean for you to get hurt. I wonder why it is that everything I do turns out wrong."

The nights grew colder as autumn approached. It was the season that Andrés and José especially liked, for the storehouses were being filled and food was prepared for the long winter months. Mother and grandmother seemed to be hurrying from sunup until long after the boys had been tucked under the quilts at night. Beans and other legumes were shelled; the corn was dried and stored away;

potatoes were dug and carried to the bins; and the winter's fuel supply was laid by.

Besides María's burdens and responsibilities of feeding and clothing her family and giving her boys religious and moral training, she had a weight of sorrow from which she could never quite escape. In the churchyard cemetery on the hill were two small graves, where two of her children lay sleeping. The first had been a little girl whose life slipped away in a mysterious illness at the age of one month. Adequate medical help was not available in the village that was isolated at certain times in winter. When epidemics came, they struck terror to the hearts of the people, especially to the parents of small children.

After the disappointment of losing her first baby, María was comforted with the birth of another child, a chubby little boy. However, her joy was not to last. When he was seven years old typhoid fever struck the village, and María's fair-headed treasure was among those who were carried up the hill to the churchyard.

According to her belief, María often entertained the idea that the spirits of her loved ones were never far away. Many masses were said and paid for to assure her that her babies were safe in heaven; but she believed, too, that they could be near her when they desired to be.

José had been five years old when his brother died, and Andrés three. Although he didn't remember his brother, Andrés had many times listened to the stories his mother and grandmother had told.

He was always conscious of the spirits, especially those who were suffering in purgatory. There was a small lake not far from the village which Andrés tried to avoid, especially when he was alone. Some of the villagers had told that when they went by that place they could hear the cries of the tormented souls in purgatory. In the years of childhood Andrés formed the impression that God was not a loving Father, but a stern ruler who was ever ready to mete out punishment.

In Spain it was a common custom for persons to dig up the bones of loved ones and take them into their homes, in an effort to bring their spirits back.

One day María went to the graveyard where the little boy was buried, and recovered his bones. She placed them in a glass container she had purchased for that purpose, then carried it back to her house and set it on the shelf above the improvised altar between some candles.

Calling Andrés and José to her, the mother said, "Tonight you are three brothers instead of two."

"What do you mean, mamma?" they asked as they looked at each other in surprise.

"I mean that tonight we have your brother with us," she explained, pointing to the bones, plainly visible in the glass container.

José and Andrés were awed and fearful in the candle-lighted room. They were relieved, however, when their mother took their brother's bones back to the cemetery the following day.

According to Spanish custom, each child has a godmother, usually a close friend of the family. María was godmother to a boy who lived in the neighboring house. Because of her long-standing friendship with little Juan's mother and the fact that she was his godmother, María had been like a second mother to the boy.

When Juan became seriously ill, his family were alarmed. María was concerned and found herself preoccupied all day with thoughts of the little boy lying in his bed, feverish and listless.

"I am going to see Juancito again," María told her mother, as she pulled her wool shawl around her head and shoulders.

"Yes, you must go," answered the grandmother; "even though there is nothing you can do to help him, perhaps you can comfort the family."

Andrés and José had gone to bed and darkness had settled over the valley. Sickness always seems worse during the dark hours of the night.

As María walked into the house, she saw the gray, drawn faces of Juan's mother and father.

"How is he?" she asked in a quiet voice.

"He is worse, María," Juan's mother answered, her eyes full of tears.

The boy's face was flushed with fever and he tossed in delirium. María was reminded of the long vigil she had passed with her own child who died, and the pain she had suffered as she helplessly watched him slip away.

María thought, "I don't believe that little Juan will make it;" but aloud she spoke words of encouragement. She went into the kitchen to fix something hot for the parents to drink.

Later, tossing on her bed, María felt that sleep would never come; her heart was with the family next door. She finally slept, but she was suddenly aroused by thinking that she heard heavy steps on the roof. In a few minutes there was a knock on the door. When she opened the bolted door, there was a member of Juancito's family to tell her that the little boy had just breathed his last.

María was certain she had heard the spirits coming for little Juan that night, and the next morning she sent someone up on the roof to see if the tiles had been broken.

One evening as the sun was setting, Andrés saw his mother donning her coat and shawl. "Mamma, where are you going?" he asked.

"I am going to the cemetery, son. You know I often go there to pray for the spirits of the poor souls in purgatory."

"May I go with you, mamma?"

He didn't fancy the cemetery at night, but he felt that he would not be afraid with his mother.

They went hand in hand along the road that led to the silent, dark church surrounded by tombstones. As María found her way to her accustomed place of prayer, Andrés did a little investigating on his own. The white stone figures and statues were eerie and grotesque by moonlight. Unconsciously Andrés found himself tiptoeing along the paths, for every crackle of a dry leaf or broken twig under his feet made him jump.

Suddenly Andrés stood petrified. He saw what appeared to be sparks of fire, apparently coming from one of the graves near where he stood. He opened his mouth to call his mother, but no sound would come. Looking around to see where she was, he could see nothing but rows of tombstones and statues. Realizing that he was lost from his mother, his next thought was to run. Heading for the road over which they had come, Andrés flew wildly down the hill, terrified with fear.

Sometimes stumbling in the darkness and catching his clothes on a fence as he crossed a field, he finally stumbled up the steps to his home, crying hysterically.

"Andrés! What is the meaning of this? Where is your mother?" Grandma was frightened at the sight of Andrés in such a condition and without his mother.

When he had recovered himself sufficiently, he tried to explain. "I got lost from mamma and saw some spirits. I was never so frightened in my life!"

The next day at school Andrés told the teacher of his harrowing experience. "There were real sparks! I saw them with my own eyes! Do you suppose it was the spirits?"

"I'm not much of a believer in spirits, lad. I imagine what you saw was phosphorus that is thrown off by old bones," his teacher explained.

"Well, whatever it was, I hope I never have to go there again at night," Andrés decided emphatically.

3

THE DREAMS OF YOUTH

"**B**REAKFAST is ready!" called María to her young sons as they hurriedly prepared for school.

Andrés and José, their faces scrubbed and their hair combed, seated themselves at the long table with the rest of the family. Steaming cereal in bowls, a cup of chocolate beside each place, and a large plate of browned potatoes in the middle of the table, along with María's homemade bread and butter, provided a hearty breakfast for sharp appetites.

María stood in the doorway and watched her boys march off to school, swinging their lunch pails. "They are good boys," she said to herself. "It is true that they are mischievous, but they are good. May God give me wisdom to make something of them."

Later, when the morning's work was finished, María told her mother, "There is no one to clean the church this week, mamma, so I am going there to sweep and dust. If the boys return before I am home, tell them to take care of their chores. They always seem to need to be reminded."

"Go along, María, and don't worry about the boys. I'll see to them and their chores. I don't know what Padre Antonio would do without you. Some of the other parishioners ought to take more interest in the church," grandma commented.

"That may be true," answered the younger woman; "but I really enjoy doing what I can for the church."

Reaching for the church keys that had been entrusted to her, she set off down the path. María, now in her middle thirties, was still slim and lithe. Although she was dressed in the long, full skirts and colored blouses customary in that village, and wore over her shoulders a fringed shawl that she also used as a head covering, her face was by no means ordinary. She had delicate features, combined with a ruddy complexion and deep blue eyes. Although she combed her hair into two braids that wound around her head, there were stray curls that would not be tamed.

"Ah! There goes María to the church," said one old woman to another as they sat spinning yarn.

"That María," commented the other; "she is always busy with something. She never has time to stop and chat."

"She is a good woman," answered the first gossip; "I've known her since she was a little girl. She hasn't had it easy, but you never hear her complain. Talk about courage, she's one that never lacks for that. She will attempt anything if she thinks it is right."

María walked on through the village, nodding and smiling at villagers she met. The breeze against her face was exhilarating, and the problems that had loomed so large the day before now seemed to diminish. While she worked in the church, moving the hard, wooden benches to clean under them, Padre Antonio came to speak to her.

"Good morning, Doña María. How are things with you today?"

"I and my family are well, padre, thank you," she answered, continuing her work.

"Doña María, if you can spare a few minutes, I would like to talk with you. There is something on my mind," the priest continued.

"Of course, padre. What is it? I am at your service."

"I am thinking of your two boys. What training are you planning to give them?" questioned the priest.

"It has always been my dream that one of my boys should have the desire and prove worthy to enter the priesthood," María confided. "Time will tell which it will be, but somehow I feel it will be the younger one, Andrés."

"I have noticed young Andrés," the padre commented. "He always seems attentive and reverent in church. You know the priesthood is a dedicated life; it will take much preparation, even now while he is small."

"Do you have some suggestions, padre?" María asked.

"Well, Doña María, I have been wondering if you would permit him to serve the church as altar boy. Since young Ramiro has gone, there has been no one. I shall be glad to train him."

"Padre, that will be wonderful! Thank you," María enthusiastically replied. "I'll talk to Andrés as soon as he comes from school."

María hurried to complete the cleaning, and she managed to be home when the boys returned from school.

"How did your classes go today?" she asked as the boys took off their caps and jackets.

"It was all right, I guess," answered José without enthusiasm. "I'll be glad, though, when I get big and don't have to go to school any more. I want to be a soldier and go to foreign places to fight for my country."

"The life of a soldier may sound exciting, my boy, but it is not an easy life. Since you have many years yet before you decide, let us see what you think when you are older," suggested the mother. "And you, Andrés, what are you going to be?"

"Maybe a farmer, mamma, I don't know," the younger boy answered pensively.

"Well, we won't worry about it yet, son. By the way, I have some news for you, Andrés. Today I was cleaning the church when Padre Antonio spoke to me about you."

"About me? What did he say?" Andrés was curious.

"He would like for you to be the altar boy like Ramiro was," María declared.

"He wants me to be altar boy?" young Andrés exclaimed.

"Yes; he says he will train you to help in the service of the church. The padre says that if you should choose to be a priest, this experience would help you," answered the mother.

"When can I start?" Andrés was eager.

"You may talk to Padre Antonio today, son. He will tell you what to do."

In a flash Andrés had his hat and jacket on again and was out the door, racing through the village and up the winding road to the church. He arrived at the church door out of breath. Before pulling the heavy door open, he suddenly realized that he did not know what he would say to the padre. He had always felt awe-stricken in the presence of the priest. Gathering courage, he pulled on the door and stepped inside.

Padre Antonio was near the front of the church, arranging some candles. At the sound of a door opening, he glanced back to see ten-year-old Andrés.

"Well, Andrés, how are you?" said the padre, coming back to where the boy was standing. "Your mother must have told you of my suggestion. Have you come to talk about your new job?"

"Yes, padre, my mother said that you wanted me."

"Come with me and I will show you what your work will be." Padre Antonio walked toward the front of the church with the boy following. "Now, you will be here early on Sunday mornings to ring the church bell. Another day I will show you how to prepare the Communion bread and wine. The candles will have to be lighted, and other duties will come later. Does it sound hard?"

"I will do the best I can, padre, and learn all that you teach me," Andrés replied.

Having been dismissed by the priest, young Andrés raced back down the hill to tell his family about his new work. He could hardly wait until the day he would begin.

The first Sunday that Andrés was to do the work of altar boy, he was out of bed before the other members of the family. Padre Antonio had said to be there early. Since the first mass was at six o'clock, he was in the church before the sun rose. Until he learned, the padre would help him prepare the bread and wine. Lighting the candles was easy, and he loved to climb into the belfry to ring the church bell.

As the first of the worshipers began to gather, Andrés helped the padre into the robes that he wore for the Sunday masses. There were ornaments and medals, which young Andrés gazed at with admiration.

"Maybe I will be a priest someday, too," he thought, "and then I can wear elegant robes like these."

Soon Andrés was performing his duties efficiently and had learned to chant responses in Latin during the mass. The winter months passed quickly and spring came again.

It was always a happy time for the boys when their grandfather came from the winter feeding grounds with their sheep. This year their mother had received word as to the day when grandfather expected to be home. José and Andrés were up early. After their breakfast had been devoured María gave them permission to go to the crest of the first hill, where they could watch for the flock to better advantage.

"I'll race you to the top," shouted José as the boys crossed the bridge and began the ascent up the other side.

They reached the brow of the hill at almost the same time, and the race was soon forgotten as they eagerly scanned the horizon for a sign of the home-coming flock.

"When will they ever come?" sighed Andrés, after a morning of waiting interspersed with rabbit chases.

The sun was now directly overhead and still there was no sign of life on the trail that led through the next valley and on up the rugged mountain in the background.

"We might as well go home for dinner," suggested the older boy. "Grandfather may not come until night or even tomorrow."

The boys ran down the hill, knowing that dinner would be ready. As they entered the house, their noses told them they were not mistaken. There was the delicious aroma of fresh bread. Garbanzos were bubbling in the iron kettle at the back of the stove. Mother was beginning to dish up the potatoes, with cream poured over them.

"What's the matter, boys? Haven't you seen anything of grandfather and the sheep yet?" María asked.

"Not a thing, mamma. Do you suppose they are really coming today?" answered José.

"Well, I wouldn't give up yet, if I were you," answered their mother. "There is the whole afternoon left. They will no doubt show up before evening."

"Are we going to have that cake for dinner?" asked Andrés.

"No, son," his mother answered. "Grandmother has made it to celebrate grandfather's arrival. He will be hungry for some good home cooking. Perhaps he will be here for supper."

After lunch the boys again climbed the hill where they could watch for grandfather and the sheep.

Late in the afternoon José strained his eyes as he thought he detected movement on the distant slopes.

"Andrés, do you see something moving on the far hill?" he asked his brother.

Andrés looked long and hard and then answered, "Yes, José, I do! Look, there are many moving objects. It is they! It is they!"

Headed down the path on a dead run, the boys finally arrived at the flock, tired and out of breath.

"Well, well, here are my boys," exclaimed grandfather. "I was wondering if you would be watching for us." He swept them both into his arms.

That evening the sheep rested in the home corral as María and her family celebrated a happy reunion. The two women had many goodies baked, and the big table was laden with savory dishes. One of María's fat hens had been prepared for the occasion. There were mashed potatoes, homemade noodles, creamed cabbage, and, as always, the delicious bread with blackberry jam. José and Andrés were careful to save room for grandma's delicious cake with mouth-watering fruit filling.

"How good to be home!" sighed grandfather as he pushed his chair to a tilting position on the two back legs. "Mother, you and María did yourselves proud on the dinner. I don't know when food has tasted better."

"We are so glad and thankful to God that you are safe home again," replied the older woman. "Tell us about your adventures the past few months."

The three older ones sat and talked of all that had happened since last grandfather had been there. José and Andrés were finally sent off to bed when sleep began to overtake them.

This summer in particular was a happy time for José and Andrés, one long to be remembered. They spent joyous, carefree days with their grandfather, herding the sheep on the hills surrounding the village.

One warm summer morning, Andrés was alone with the flock, and there was nothing to break the stillness but the bleating of the sheep. A vulture swooped near him a few times and then glided down into a meadow nearby. The boy sat on a large rock above the grassy clearing where the sheep were grazing contentedly.

"What would it be like to be a priest?" Andrés thought.

Carried into action by his imagination, he jumped to his feet, stood on the rock where he had been sitting, and began to preach with all vigor the sermon he had heard Padre Antonio give the previous Sunday. So dynamic and eloquent did he become that the sheep left off eating and looked in the direction of the enthusiastic young fellow.

Absorbed in his sermonizing, Andrés was unaware that his grandfather had walked up behind him. "What is the young pastor up to now?" the older man chided. "Do you think the sheep need to be reminded of their sins?"

"Oh, grandfather! You surprised me!" Andrés quickly descended from his pedestal with an embarrassed grin.

"Is it the priesthood that you are aspiring to, my lad?" asked the white-haired old man.

"I don't know, grandfather. Mother wants me to be a priest, and Padre Antonio says it is the most certain way to please God."

"It is a worthy ambition, Andrés, but do with your life what your heart tells you. Now I think your mother is waiting lunch for you."

4

BEGINNING TRAINING
FOR THE PRIESTHOOD

YEARS came and went. Grandfather passed to his rest and grandmother grew more feeble. She spent most of her time in her chair, mending or knitting.

One evening when Andrés was thirteen, María announced to the family, gathered at the evening meal, "I heard today that some famous missionaries are coming this way. It is believed that they will be holding meetings in a nearby village which is more central."

"I have always wanted to see and hear some missionaries," spoke up Andrés. "Can we go, mamma?"

"If it isn't too far away, of course we'll go, son. I will ask Padre Antonio more about it when I see him."

Several days later María received definite word that two missionaries would hold meetings for a week at the church in the next village, four miles away. The meetings were scheduled to begin on a Sunday, the first one at five o'clock in the morning.

On the appointed day, long before sunrise, María, José, and Andrés were on their way to the church. It took almost two hours for them to walk the four miles, and they arrived on time. Andrés sat with his eyes glued to the speaker, deeply impressed by the stories of adventure.

On the homeward journey that evening he confided to his mother, "If I could be a missionary like that man, then I would like to be a priest. Do you think I could?"

"I don't know, son; but we can talk to one of them about it. Shall we do it tomorrow?"

The next morning they journeyed to the church again, for the boys were anxious not to miss a meeting. As they entered the building, one of the missionaries was near the door to greet them. "I need someone to be my bell ringer. Which of you two boys would like the job?" he asked.

"I would," offered Andrés, "or do you want to, José?" he asked, turning to his brother.

"You go ahead," the older boy replied, thinking that the task might be beneath the dignity of a fifteen-year-old like himself.

"All right, then, you will ring the bell before every meeting," the man instructed Andrés.

Later in the week one of the missionaries found occasion to talk to María. "You have two fine boys there, señora; what education do you plan to give them?"

"I have been planning to speak with you," María answered. "The older boy seems to be interested in a military life, but the younger one—I would like for him to be a priest."

"I have noticed him during these meetings," continued the missionary. "He does seem religiously inclined. How old is he?"

"Andrés will soon be fourteen. What arrangements could be made for my boy to enter a seminary?"

"If he is almost fourteen, then I would suggest that he

enter the seminary this summer, for a new class starts in August. If you like, I will submit his name and you will receive instructions as to when he should come."

"Thank you, padre. It will be a great sacrifice for me to send my boy away, but I am willing if that is God's will," María added wistfully.

"May I give you a word of advice, señora," the missionary added. "Begin now to prepare him for the hardships and sacrifices ahead. Give him poor food occasionally. You know the food at the seminary isn't too good at times. It will help him not to be dissatisfied if he becomes accustomed to plain food before he goes."

In the days that followed Andrés thought often of what it would be like to leave home and live at a school with other boys.

"You will come to see me, won't you, mamma?" he asked his mother one day.

"It would be a long way for me to come," María answered evasively.

The question caused the mother sudden pain as she remembered the missionary telling her that it would be better for her never to come, lest she cause the boy to be homesick. María treasured every day that she had with Andrés in the months before he was to leave for the seminary. Many nights she lay awake thinking of and dreading the day when she would tell him good-by. Only her deep conviction that it was her religious duty enabled her to carry the plan through.

The letter arrived from the seminary giving instructions when Andrés was to be there. Final arrangements were made, and María prepared her son's clothes. On Sunday, the day before the boy's departure, the family went as usual to the church on the hill. It would be Andrés's last service as altar boy. As Padre Antonio began the mass, many eyes were on the youth. These people, who had watched him grow up and had become accustomed to his serving in the services, were saddened at the thought of his leaving.

When the last of the parishioners had left the church, the padre spoke to Andrés. "Well, my boy, I am going to miss you. The life that you have chosen will not be an easy one, but I am sure that you will succeed. Don't let anything discourage you. Perhaps the next time I see you your course will be finished and you will be here to celebrate your first mass as Padre Andrés."

"Thank you, padre, for all you have done and your patience with me. I hope I shall not disappoint you." Then, as Andrés walked toward the door, he added, "I guess I should be going now."

"Good-by, Andrés. God bless you!"

The boy walked slowly down the hill in serious thought. He knew every inch of this country, for he could remember no other environment but this village and its happy, carefree life. He had been sheltered from the hard blows of life by the loving care of his mother. He almost wished that he could forget the idea of going away to school; he would rather stay here in the good life that he knew.

As María looked at the face of the sleeping boy the following morning, her heart almost froze. Memory after memory raced before her mind's eye—the days when she had rocked him in his cradle, the many times she had kissed away his tears. He was still a little boy to her.

"Andrés, it is time to awaken; it is morning." She touched his forehead lightly and his eyes opened.

As he realized that this was the last morning at home, the morning they had been planning for, he jumped out of bed. With morning came fresh courage, and Andrés was eager to be on the way to have his first train ride and meet what life had to offer.

His mother had carefully laid out his clothes the night before, and when he appeared, dressed ready to go, María surveyed him proudly. His suit was brown velveteen with tapering pants, his white shirt had a Peter Pan collar, and his close-fitting hat was brown to match his suit.

"Come, son; have your breakfast," grandma said, as she set the steaming cereal and hot chocolate on the table. There were fried potatoes and eggs along with the usual thick slices of bread and newly churned butter. "María, you must eat, too. You have a long trip ahead," continued the older woman.

In the last moments before leaving, María led the boy into the little chapel adorned with images and candles. They knelt together at the humble altar and recited the rosary. María said a special prayer to the Virgin Mary for her youngest child who was going far away.

"José, it is time to get the animals ready. Bring them to the door," María called to the older boy.

Andrés took a last look through the house while his brother saddled the horse and burro that they had borrowed from his uncle for the trip to the station. In a short time the bags were tied on and Andrés told his grand-mother good-by.

"*Adiós, mi abuelita*," he said as the old woman wrapped him in her arms.

Tears rolled down her cheeks as she gave him her bene-diction. "God bless you, my boy. Don't forget us. We will say prayers for you every day."

There was a lump in his throat as Andrés bade his brother good-by. Soon he and his mother were riding down the road on the animals.

The familiar streets, the houses, and the church—all faded into the background as the travelers rode along the dusty road. It was a ride of six hours over hills, through valleys, and across small creeks.

Nearing the bank of a small stream, Andrés asked, "Mother, let's eat our lunch here. It is such a pretty place."

"Very well, Andrés, we will stop here. We will not be able to tarry long, though. It will rush us to catch the train."

The tired animals drank long from the sparkling stream and then munched the green grass growing in the shade of tall trees. Andrés, after eating his lunch, pulled off his shoes and stockings and waded in the cold water. The day was hot and the travelers delighted in a brief respite from the heat.

"It is time to be on our way," María called to the boy.

"I'm coming, mother," he answered, as he hurriedly put on his stockings and shoes and again mounted his burro.

María on the stout brown horse and Andrés on the shaggy burro made their way over the narrow mountain paths, urging the animals to go faster, lest they miss the train.

"Look, mother, the train is already there!" Andrés called to his mother in excitement.

The station platform was swarming with people. The train, with steam coming from the engine, stood ready to pull out. When the animals had been tied to a nearby hitching post, Andrés and his mother took his bags and headed for the train.

"Pardon me, señora, could you be the mother of Andrés Díaz?" a man in clerical collar asked.

"Yes, I am María de Díaz, at your service," María answered.

"I am Padre Jerónimo. I am in charge of the boys who are going to the seminary. I have the name of your son on my list."

"I am happy to have the pleasure of knowing you, padre. This is my son, Andrés." Then turning to the boy, she continued, "Andrés, this is Padre Jerónimo. He is going to take care of you until you reach the school. I hope you will be very obedient to him."

"Yes, mother, of course."

As the call was made for passengers to climb aboard, María embraced her son. She had tried to brace herself for this moment and had fully intended to save her tears for the lonesome ride home; but the moment of parting seemed to tear her heart, and the tears came.

Although young Andrés could not comprehend the long years that would stand between him and his mother, still this farewell seemed more than he could bear. The final moment could be postponed no longer, and the youth stepped up into the railroad car. He watched and waved as long as he could see his mother; but when the train rounded a curve, she was lost from sight.

Andrés found his seat and sat quietly for a long time. A lonesome feeling crept over him and he longed to be riding back over the hills with his mother toward home. After a time, however, his attention focused on his surroundings. The other boys, twenty-five of them, were making things lively. It was a motley group, because each youth was dressed differently. It was the custom for each village or community to have its typical costume. Since the boys came from different villages, there was an unusual array of clothing styles.

"Hello, what is your name?" A pleasant-faced boy with tawny hair and blue eyes spoke in a friendly manner.

"Andrés," he answered. "What's yours?"

"My name is Felipe. I've been on this train since last night."

The two boys found a mutual understanding at once, and this was the beginning of a long and deep friendship. Felipe gave pertinent information about his family. "My father is a fisherman and we live on the north coast," he said. "There are six children in our family, but I'm the oldest. Sometimes my father takes me with him on fishing trips, and that's what I really like. What does your father do?"

Andrés looked at his feet. "My father lives in South America, and we haven't seen him for a long, long time." Then he brightened as he continued, "But my mother and brother and I live with my grandmother. We have fields of grain, potatoes, garbanzos, and other foodstuffs. We have sheep and cows, too; but since grandfather died, my uncle keeps our sheep with his flocks."

The group of prospective students were on the train two nights. Riding became tiresome the third day as they neared their destination. "It is time to get your things ready to leave the train," the priest announced to the group. "We will be there within half an hour."

Excitement prevailed as each boy gathered his belongings and watched out the window for the station to come into view. Andrés noticed that this country was not particularly different from his native hills. Mountains could be seen, although they were not as rugged as those around his home.

A bus met the group at the station, and they were soon on their way to the ancient monastery that would be their home for the next five years.

"What do you suppose it will be like?" Andrés asked.

"I don't know," the other boy answered. "I feel scared inside, now that we are so close to the monastery."

As the bus bumped along the rough roads, each boy watched intently for the first glimpse of the school.

"Is that it?" one boy called.

"Yes, here we are," answered Padre Jerónimo.

The gray stone buildings stood in a group in a valley, surrounded by beautiful trees, rolling hills, and a green meadow. The large buildings, huddled in a circle, were medieval in appearance. As one looked at them, he felt that time was turning back hundreds of years.

"It looks like an old castle from my history book," Andrés confided to Felipe.

The noisy, laughing boys bounded through the stone archway, but became suddenly awed and hushed. They faced priests in long robes, who were slowly pacing the tomblike corridors with solemn countenance. Andrés and his companions soon learned that they were expected to go in single file through the halls.

"You there, you in the brown suit," one of the robed figures spoke to Andrés in a sharp voice, "tone your voice down. This is not the place for frivolity."

The boys were taken to the third floor of a building that faced a beautiful patio. Here they found a large room with rows and rows of narrow beds. Beside each bed stood something that resembled a bookcase with shelves. On the top of each set of shelves was a washpan.

"Andrés Díaz, this will be your bed. Felipe, come to the other side of the room with me."

"Oh, please, padre," Andrés spoke up. "Felipe and I are friends. There is a vacant place here next to me. Won't you please let him stay here?"

"Young man, in this place you take orders and do not give them. Come with me, Felipe."

Andrés felt hot tears welling into his eyes. Why should this new padre be so cross? He hadn't done anything wrong. Separated from Felipe, he felt alone and frightened.

That night, tossing on his narrow cot, with a hard straw tick for a mattress, Andrés thought of his home. He longed for the light touch of his mother's lips on his forehead as she kissed him and tucked him and his brother in bed.

5

SEMINARY DISCIPLINE

WHEN the rising bell rang at five o'clock the next morning, Andrés awoke with a start, surprised and frightened to find himself in strange surroundings. Somehow he had expected to wake up in the bedroom he shared with José. Collecting his thoughts, he jumped out of bed and pulled on his clothes, anxious to give the padre in charge no reason to scold him.

Of the several hundred students in the school, sixty-five were in the new class. At five thirty o'clock, when Andrés and his group formed a line to go to the church for mass, he managed to walk with Felipe. In a low voice, Felipe asked, "What do you think of things by now?"

"It isn't at all what I thought it would be like," Andrés answered.

"No whispering there, you two!" the padre spoke in a loud voice over the heads of the group. Arriving at the church, which was near the other buildings, each boy was given a place to kneel where he could recite the rosary. They were instructed to remain there in prayer until they were told to rise. Although Andrés had been taught from infancy to say prayers each day, he had never spent a half hour at a time on his knees.

"I wonder how long they will make us stay here," he said to himself after fifteen minutes had gone by.

When at last the word was given to arise, his knees were aching. Every hour of the day was regimented, with but little time for recreation. There was a playground behind the buildings where the short periods of play were spent in ball games or other activity. In the buildings there was no laughing, joking, or unnecessary talking. These students were to learn discipline in its severest form.

When several days had passed, one of the teachers announced: "Every day an 'accuser' will be appointed from among you. He will be given a notebook and paper and during the day will write down every misdemeanor and the name of the guilty party. At an appointed time each evening the accuser will read his list and punishments will be meted out."

One evening, shortly thereafter, the accuser was reading his list when Andrés was startled to hear his own name. "Andrés Díaz—while standing in line waiting for lunch turned around and grinned at the boy behind him."

"Andrés, to teach you the seriousness of the life you are learning, you will be required to repeat the Lord's Prayer twenty-five times at mass tomorrow morning," the padre said.

Andrés did not reply, but resentment rose up in him. There was nothing he could do, however, but comply and receive his punishment.

On another evening the accuser read the names of Felipe and Andrés together. "These two boys were seen alone in the patio during the recreation period."

"But, padre," spoke up Andrés, "what is wrong in walking with someone through the patio?"

"Young man," the padre exclaimed, "who gave you permission to try to defend yourself? Because you have answered back, your punishment will be doubled. In this school, not even the appearance of evil is allowed. From now on, you stay with the group." Then continuing, he said, "Felipe, you will be given no dessert for two days, but Andrés will be four days without any."

By now the boys had come to look forward to such simple treats as a spoonful of honey after a meal. The meals were poorly cooked, flat, and tasteless, and frequently there was not enough food to satisfy the appetites of growing boys.

After a few weeks of the stern discipline, Andrés was resigned to accept whatever came. He no longer remonstrated over unjust punishment, even though sometimes he was not guilty in the remotest way. During the Lenten season there were many days of fasting when the food was measured out in ounces. The boys, who were not old enough to fast with genuine religious spirit, suffered real hunger. Mealtime and food became almost an obsession. Also during these times of special religious periods, they were made to kneel in prayer for longer and longer periods until they were on their knees two and three hours at a time. After these occasions, Andrés would have difficulty in walking because his knees became painfully swollen.

One morning, while the boys were making their beds, Raul, who had come from a remote mountain district, shouted as he looked out a window, "Look at the strange animal coming down the street! It has eyes and makes a funny noise."

When the other boys ran to look, they laughed to discover that Raul's "animal" was only a car. At that moment the superior walked in the door. "No dessert today!" he decreed.

The boys' faces fell, remembering that one of the group had peeked in the kitchen that morning and brought back the word that there was honey for dinner.

While the boys stood in line for dinner, a superior motioned to one of the boys, "Santiago, come with me."

Santiago followed the priest to another room. Later on one of the boys asked, "What happened to Santiago? Where is he?" Santiago had been sent home for a misdemeanor and was not able to bid his friends good-by. He had been ushered out unceremoniously, and loaded on the bus for his home.

When winter came, the old stone buildings became uncomfortably cold. Since there was no heating system in the chill, damp buildings, the boys could only put on more clothes to keep warm. Before retiring each night, every boy filled his washbasin and placed it on his shelf beside his bed. Many times ice formed in the pans overnight, and in the morning they would have to break the ice in order to wash their face and hands.

Summertime was more agreeable, and if a boy passed his examinations he enjoyed a vacation from classes and worked in the gardens and fields behind the school. Boys who did not pass the examinations spent the summer making up their work so that they could continue with their class the next term.

Monotonous days dragged on, and Andrés somehow

accustomed himself to the heavy program of studies and the strict discipline. Three years of monastery life brought him to his seventeenth year. One day Felipe found Andrés and told him exciting news. "Andrés, guess what! I received a letter today from home and my father and mother are coming to visit me this weekend! How will I ever wait!"

"That's wonderful, Felipe," the other boy answered. "I wish—" but he didn't finish the sentence. Andrés knew that his mother had no way to make such a long trip; but she wrote him faithfully, and each letter took him back again in spirit to the home he loved.

There was a special reception room at the entrance to the monastery where students received their visitors—the few that came. Visitors were never allowed inside the school proper.

On Sunday when Felipe was called to the reception room, Andrés was seized with such a longing to see his mother, he almost decided to run off and find his way back home. He dispelled the thought, however, realizing that it would be a great disappointment to his mother if he returned home a failure.

"I think I'll slip down and see if I can catch a glimpse of Felipe's mother and father. I wonder what they look like," he said to himself.

Quickly and quietly Andrés slipped down the two flights of stairs, through a long hall, and to a door that opened into a small room at the entrance of the school. Felipe was sitting between a kind-faced man and a sweet-looking woman. They were all talking and smiling. Without having been noticed, Andrés slowly made his way down the dreary, silent hall. His heart felt as empty as the cold, tomblike corridors. The life that he had known as a boy seemed to have been in another world, a rosy, warm world, where love and affection had enveloped him. Now his spirit seemed to be dead, for he seldom heard a kind word or received an approving smile. During the three years he had learned discipline. He could walk in line, stand at attention without turning his head, and be quiet unless he was spoken to. He ate his meals automatically and without relish.

As for his desire to be a priest, he hardly knew his own heart; probably fear of doing anything different was his chief motivation. At times he felt that he was little more than a machine, performing his appointed duties at set times. At last, the day came for the graduating exercises. The first five years of his studies were over.

One of his teachers in talking to him said, "Andrés, you have done well here. Now almost half of your training is over, and we feel you will succeed. It takes some steel in the character to persevere and become a priest. You have seen how few of your original class members are still here."

"Yes, padre, I was thinking that there were sixty-five of us to begin with, but now we are only fifteen. I sometimes wonder that I am still here."

"The next year will be the real test," the padre continued. "You will have to be very strong; you must never consider giving up. When your superiors seem hard and unreasonable, remember that it is for a purpose. The weak, vacillating ones must be eliminated. There are actually few people who have the material to become priests, but I believe you are one of the few. Don't ever give up."

Andrés appreciated the words of encouragement from his teacher. Now a young man almost twenty years of age, he felt mature and able to think for himself. Since his faith was the only true one, what greater dedication of life could he choose?

Excitement prevailed on the weekend of the closing exercises. Many of the parents arrived to enjoy the program and visit with their sons. Again Andrés found himself among the few who had no visitors. Somehow the young man had entertained a faint hope that someone from home would arrive at the last moment, but his name had never been called to come to the visitors' room. He sat in an almost empty dormitory while the reception room downstairs buzzed with excitement.

"I'm so sorry, friend, that your family couldn't come," Felipe told him in sincere sympathy.

"It doesn't matter; I knew they wouldn't be here," Andrés answered, almost sharply.

"Why don't you come down and visit with my folks?" his friend asked. "Mother and father would be happy to see you."

Andrés forced a smile. "Thanks, Felipe, you're a friend. I appreciate the thought, really I do; but I think I'll stay here."

Felipe reluctantly left, thinking as he walked down the stairs, "Strange thing, after all these years, he's never had a single visitor. Looks like his mother could find some way to get here. He always speaks of his people with deep affection and respect; but actually, I know little about his family."

Andrés wondered why he was the only one who had never had a visitor. He knew his mother was poor, but he had uncles who could help her with the fare. What was the real reason why she had never come to see him?

6

HARDSHIPS AT HOME

THE day that Andrés left for the seminary, María had stood as one transfixed, watching the train as it grew smaller and finally rounded a curve and was lost from sight. The tears that had flowed easily a few minutes before now dried up at the fount. Her eyes were dry and smarting. Silently her lips moved. "God knows I have done my best; I have given Him my son. I had no more precious gift."

Mechanically she untied the animals, fastened the reins of the burro to the saddle of the horse she was to ride, mounted, and turned in the direction of home.

"María, my dear, you must stop brooding," her mother said to her one day some time later. "You have hardly smiled since Andrés left."

"I'm sorry, mother, I don't want to make everyone's life gloomy. It's just that—well, sometimes, I wonder why I ever sent him away. He was so young; he didn't know what it all meant. I wish I could be sure that it was the right thing to do."

"Don't torment yourself with such thoughts, child. You know we have always been taught that a priest in the family brings salvation to the household. You will be glad and proud someday when people call your son 'padre.'"

Life has a way of going on in spite of everything. The

responsibilities of the farm kept María physically busy, at least. That autumn the garbanzos, an important food in the diet of every Spaniard, along with lentils and other vegetables, had to be harvested. The mother worked long hours, and José helped her even more than usual, sensing his mother's sorrow. When the last of the harvest was stored in the cellar and the sacks of wheat were ready to be taken to the mill, grandmother began the needlework that kept their hands busy during the winter months.

"What are you planning for José to do?" grandmother ventured to ask María. Since Andrés was gone, María had deliberately postponed a decision concerning José's future. He was sixteen now, and in one more year he would finish the village school.

"That is a question I am not anxious to think about," replied María. "He still seems bent on a military career, and I suppose that will be his decision. I'm glad he can be with us at least one more year."

"Where are you, mamma?" called José, as he flung the door open, breathless with excitement.

María hurried to José. "Here I am, son. What is it?"

"There is news, mamma; everyone is talking about it. They say that the rebel armies are taking control of more and more villages in the north. The government is calling for volunteers for military service. I must go." His words tumbled out in rapid succession.

Fear gripped María's heart, for she knew the day had been postponed as long as possible. José's restless spirit would be quiet no longer; he would respond to this urgent appeal to his patriotism.

"Very well, José. If this is what you really want, you must go. However, I have one request to make."

"What is it, mamma?" José asked with respect.

"It is that you enter a military school and be trained properly. I cannot think of you rushing into the fighting with no training."

José was glad to comply with this request. In fact, his ambition had long been to be an officer under the Spanish flag.

Once more María prepared a son to leave the home nest. When he had gone, home was almost unbearably empty and quiet. There was the routine work on the farm, but the woman no longer kept so many animals. With only herself and grandmother, it wasn't necessary to store so much food for the winter, so the two women spent some of their time sewing for relatives.

One day the village was filled with alarm. "Did you say that the rebels are actually expected to invade our village?" María asked the question, for she could scarcely believe her ears.

"Yes," her cousin answered. "They have been pilfering and wrecking town after town as they come down from the north. They are not more than sixty kilometers away right now. We must all leave our homes or take the chance of being killed."

María hurried home to talk the situation over with grandmother. "Mother, we must prepare to leave our home. It is no longer safe to stay here. We are in the path of the rebels, who are coming down from the north."

"But María," answered the old lady, wringing her hands, "how can we go? Where will we go?"

"Don't you remember our cousins, Helena and Mateo, who live in that small mountain village about thirty kilometers away? Since it can be reached only by a mountain trail, it will be much safer there," María assured her. "We will have to walk, though," she added.

It was a painful ordeal to leave behind all the earthly possessions which meant so much to them. María wondered if and when she would ever see them again. As the two women began the ascent up the first hill, leaving their beloved village behind, their hearts were sad. They were dressed in full, long skirts, with dark shawls around their heads and shoulders. María had tied a few things in a wool blanket. They could use the blanket for protection if they should encounter bad weather. They wore extra clothing rather than carry it.

The first day went fairly well. Not too many miles were covered, because the aged grandmother tired easily and it was necessary to stop often for rest. The first night they were fortunate to come to a humble dwelling beside the road where an old man and woman welcomed them. In the morning, after a simple but nourishing breakfast, María again encouraged her mother to venture out on the trail. The old lady was stiff and sore from her exertions of the previous day, and she found the going harder. Since they were beginning the hardest part of their journey, María was genuinely alarmed over their situation. She realized that grandmother was not going to be able to walk the miles that lay between them and their destination. At the rate they were going, they would be many days on the road. In the afternoon, fearing that they would not even reach shelter by nightfall, María in desperation said to her mother, "Mamma, I am going to stoop down and I want you to get on my back. I am going to carry you."

"No, child, you are not strong enough. Why didn't I stay and face the rebels?"

"Nonsense, mother. I would never have left you there. You know that. I can carry you by resting occasionally, and we can go much faster. After all, you don't weigh much any more."

Somehow María managed to carry the bundle and her mother. She moved along as fast as possible, stopping to rest when her strength ebbed. When, at the journey's end, they reached the farmhouse of their relatives, María was exhausted.

Helena was standing in the doorway when the two bedraggled travelers approached. She spoke to her husband, "Mateo, do you recognize these people coming up the road? They are two women! They must have come a long way."

Helena greeted the travelers, "Good afternoon; won't you come in?"

"Pardon me, señora," ventured María. "Aren't you Helena? I am María de Díaz. This is mother."

"María! Auntie! Whatever has happened? How did you get here?" Helena could hardly believe her eyes.

"It is a long story, Helena. We will tell you in time. First, is there a place for mother? The trip has been too much for her."

In a short time, with Helena's warm hospitality and good care, María was herself again. Grandmother never completely recovered from the exhaustion and hardships of their trek over the mountains.

One morning Mateo came into the house with serious news. "You can be thankful that you are here instead of in your own village, María. They tell me that the rebels have pilfered the entire countryside, wrecking buildings and burning some."

"God has been good to us," María answered, but her heart was heavy at the thought of their beautiful little village in ruins. María and her mother settled down to the routine of life on Helena and Mateo's farm. They were given a room and made comfortable.

One morning, while grandmother was propped up in a chair near the fire, and María and Helena were preparing vegetables for dinner, María said, "We must get in touch with my sons. Andrés and José will be frantic when they hear what has happened to our village. I must give them the assurance that mother and I are safe."

7

THROUGH ORDEAL
AND TEST

WHEN Andrés heard his name at mail call in the seminary, he was happy and excited. Weeks had passed since he had heard from his mother and grandmother as to their safety during the civil war. It was a relief to see a letter in his mother's writing. Hastily tearing open the envelope, he read:

"MY DEAR SON,

"As you may have heard, the people from our village have had to flee from the invading armies from the north. Somehow, God helped your grandmother and me to escape and we arrived safely here at cousin Helena's in the mountains. They have offered to share their home with us as long as we need it. May God richly reward them.

"José is doing well in the military school. He writes me occasionally. I am praying that all the trouble in our country will be settled before he finishes his training. I cannot bear to think of him in the fighting.

"It is a comfort to me to know that you are in God's hands. I pray for you every day. Do not fret yourself for us. We are safe and comfortable. Grandmother is failing in health. I do not know how much longer she will be with us.

"I thought of you at your graduation. I am proud that you have been faithful and are finishing your course.

                              "Lovingly, your mother."

After reading his mother's letter, Andrés was lost in thought. He could no longer enjoy thinking of his mother and grandmother in their cozy home in the village. As he wondered if their house was standing, the old urge to return home took hold on his heart. He needed to go and look after his mother and grandmother. All through that day he toyed with the idea; but toward evening he knew that he had taken a road from which there could be no turning and no detours.

Soon after the graduation exercises, the fifteen young men who had finished their first five years of training made plans to leave the old stone buildings to which they had grown accustomed. Andrés had heard fantastic stories of the novitiate training. It was considered the real test of a candidate for the priesthood, for his character and mental endurance would be put in the crucible. In his own mind he had little doubt but that he could stand the test. He felt that he had come to the place where he could stand anything. However, in the months to follow, he was to discover that there is a limit to human endurance.

The small group that remained of the original class made the journey by train to the new school. The group of men were much more serious than were the boys who made that journey five years before. During much of the trip Andrés was occupied with his prayer books, or he gazed out the window at the varied landscape. A few hours before the group reached their destination, they left the beautiful mountainous country behind and found only miles of desert stretching before them. The heat in the unventilated car became stifling.

"Well, what do you think of the country?" Felipe asked Andrés as he sat down beside his friend.

"I have been wondering if there is a living thing in this desert. If the outside is as hot as the inside of this train, I doubt if anyone or anything could survive," Andrés responded.

"We are supposed to be only two hours away from our destination," Felipe informed his friend. "I'm wondering if this is the kind of country we will live in for the next year."

"If we arrive in two hours, we won't have long to wait before we find out," returned Andrés.

The two friends presented a contrast in appearance. Felipe, who had been the tawny-haired, blue-eyed boy when he and Andrés first met, was now a handsome, tall young man, whose blue eyes reflected sincerity and friendliness. The blond hair that had been so tousled and unruly when he was a lad, was now tamed in even waves. By contrast, Andrés had dark hair with stray curls that sometimes sought their own way. His eyes were still the same honest blue. Fine features reflected the integrity and good character that had developed in his life as the result of María's careful rearing. Andrés was shorter than his friend Felipe, and of a rather slight build.

In due time the train came to a stop in the hot, dusty village where they would spend the next year. Instead of stone buildings, such as they had been accustomed to, Andrés and Felipe found the houses and business places built of adobe bricks the color of the ground. Little vegetation could be seen, for only here and there a puny tree which someone had pampered gave relief to the monotonous landscape. The people seemed as lifeless and withered as the surroundings. Indeed, life seemed to stand still under the blistering heat of the afternoon. Even the village dogs were too sleepy to bother to bark at the strangers who walked through their streets.

"Señor, can you please tell us which way the seminary is?" one of Andrés's companions asked a bystander.

"Keep going straight north on the next street and you will come to it," the man answered.

As they approached the end of the street, Andrés saw a large, rectangular brick building, standing without a shade tree near it. He and his companions were admitted and shown to their new quarters. In contrast to the previous seminary, where the students lived in one large room, this school furnished each young man with a small private room. Andrés found himself in a cubicle just large enough to accommodate a small table and one chair, and a narrow bed with wooden slats upon which a thin straw mat had been placed. There was a small window, but it was situated too near the ceiling to offer a view of the out-of-doors. He was told that there were no keys; in fact, it was against the rules to lock your room. It must always be open to the inspection of the "accuser," the one whose job it was to watch for misdemeanors and faults.

Almost immediately Andrés found himself initiated into the new life. He learned that the first fifteen days would be spent in preparing to wear the priestly robe. These fifteen days were devoted primarily to prayer and solitary meditation, with no visiting or talking allowed. Andrés had long been accustomed to spending hours on his knees; but until now prayers and religious exercises had been performed in a group more or less as a matter of form. Now it was to be a very personal matter in which each person must learn to develop his own spiritual exercises and thus rise above earthly desires and thoughts.

When the special day arrived when these new candidates would take the robe, Andrés was trembling with excitement. He considered this a milepost in his career. Since conversation was forbidden, lest it drag the mind from the spiritual sphere, Andrés could not confide in Felipe. But when they passed each other in the halls, they did exchange understanding glances, and their mutual understanding was a strength to both young men.

The impressive ceremony began with a mass conducted by the father superior, in which the fifteen candidates chanted the responses. As the rosary was said, each young man fingered his own rosary. At the moment when the black robe was placed on Andrés, he knew in his heart that he would someday be a padre. Yes, his mother, brother, and relatives would see him as Padre Andrés.

During the months that followed, Andrés passed through fiery ordeals in learning self-abnegation. Through constant supervision, with accusers always on the watch, he was taught to consider every infringement of the rules as a sin. One evening the accuser reported that Andrés had been frivolous. He had looked behind him and smiled at one of his classmates as they filed into class.

"As a punishment you will eat your breakfast on your knees," announced the superior.

At meals, no one was permitted to ask food for himself; that would be a denial of true humility. Instead, he must sit patiently, hoping the one on his right would notice that he was out of food, tap his wine bottle with his knife, and say, "My friend here needs some more soup," or whatever he imagined was desired.

On one occasion Andrés was missed in the serving of the food. The student on his right was occupied with other thoughts and forgot to see if he needed anything. Andrés sat, watching the others eat, hoping someone would notice that his plate was empty; but the meal was finished and everyone rose to leave without Andrés's having had a bit of food. He had only his wine, which was always set at each place before the meal.

Students were not allowed to be together, and students found in pairs were immediately suspected of evil thoughts or actions. Only the menial tasks, necessary to the maintenance of the institution, were performed in groups. Occasionally all the students were taken in a group to the country. After the strenuous days in the confines of the monastery, it was a great relief to spend a day in the nearby hills. One warm day they hiked a considerable distance, and everyone hoped to find a stream of water. Finally they came upon a rippling brook.

The superior turned to one of the students, asking, "Are you thirsty? Would you like a drink?"

"Oh, yes, padre," answered the unsuspecting young man.

"You know nothing of self-mortification," answered the superior harshly; "you have not begun to learn the lesson of denying self. You do not deserve a drink."

Turning to another of the group, the superior asked again, "Wouldn't you like some water? You must be very thirsty."

The second one replied warily, "No, thank you, padre," although his throat was parched and dry.

"You are a liar!" cried the angry superior. "You have answered No only to appear sanctimonious. You do not deserve a drink, either."

Turning to Andrés, the superior asked again, "How about you? Are you thirsty? Do you want a drink?"

Searching his mind frantically for the right answer, Andrés responded respectfully, "Just as you wish, padre."

His face flushed, the irate priest uttered another scathing rebuke, "You have no mind or decision of your own. You are not worthy!"

The group trudged on in thirst, no one daring to ask for water.

There were regular periods of "self-accusations," when students were asked to confess publicly their faults and weaknesses. Since there was little opportunity for serious sins, the young men would search their minds for some remote thought or action that might possibly have a bearing on their spiritual condition. The sermons and lectures concentrated on the punishments that await the wicked, the condition of man in death, and the necessity of having the mind completely free of worldly thoughts and ambitions.

The new technique in developing the conscience had a profound effect on the majority of the students. Andrés began to experience the deepest mental torture. He had cast everything behind him in his dedication, and now he began to realize that a sinless life was something he was forever groping and reaching out for but which he could never quite attain. At times he felt he could not even save his own soul, let alone learning to save others. Night after night he lay awake on his hard cot, tormented with the thought that the fires of hell awaited him. God seemed to be a cruel judge who was anxious to condemn the struggling sinner. So many days had passed since the young man smiled or had a happy thought, that the whole world seemed to be dark and gloomy. In this state of mind, Andrés sometimes felt that he would eventually lose his reason.

It was not unusual for the students to arise in the middle of the night, seek out one of the superiors, and confess some small infringement that had come to mind, in the hope that this act would silence the tormenting conscience. Each student was given instruments of self-discipline. Andrés had a "disciplina," or cat-o'-nine-tails, made of twisted and waxed rope, reinforced at the ends with other rope. In the privacy of his own room, he would bare his back and whip himself in an effort to rid his soul of sin and obtain indulgence.

There were periods when the group, including the superiors, stood in a circle with bare backs. Each one had a whip in his hand, and they chanted in unison the verses of the fifty-first psalm to a sad and mournful tune while the lashes fell to the beat of the rhythm:

> "Have mercy upon me, O God, according to Thy loving-
>   kindness:
>   According unto the multitude of Thy tender mercies
>   blot out my transgressions.
>   Wash me throughly from mine iniquity, and cleanse me
>   from my sin.
>   For I acknowledge my transgressions: and my sin is
>   ever before me. . . .
>   Purge me with hyssop, and I shall be clean:
>   Wash me, and I shall be whiter than snow."

The sting of the whips was sharp, and blood flew from the backs to the floor and walls.

Andrés became obsessed in his search for pardon and salvation. His dreams were haunted by his fear of hell and death. For the first time, the novices were now given Bibles and taught how to use them. However, only certain portions, the Psalms and the life of Christ, were studied. During this time of mental confusion, Andrés found comfort in the study of the Bible. He found that the New Testament made the gospel simple.

He read Romans 5:1: "Therefore being justified by faith, we have peace with God through our Lord Jesus Christ." Again in Romans 8:32, he read: "He that spared not His own Son, but delivered Him up for us all, how shall He not with Him also freely give us all things?"

Andrés could not reconcile these thoughts with his own conception of God. When he spoke of it to one of the superiors, the older man said firmly, "Young man, do not try to make your own interpretation of Scripture. Rome has explained the Scriptures for us; Rome is the only authority."

Excepting for one day of the week, when four hours were allowed for conversation, it was permissible to speak to a fellow student only during an hour-and-a-half period a day. The remainder of the time was to be spent in silent meditation, prayer, or study.

Another instrument of self-torture that Andrés used was a *cilicio*, a belt two inches wide made of small loops of wire, the ends of each loop pointing inward a quarter of an inch to prick the wearer. It could be worn around the bare waist or above the knee, tightening and entering the flesh when the wearer was in a kneeling position.

Five more of the group dropped out during the year of novitiate. Some of them left for their homes, broken in health and spirit, unfit for any other walk of life. Somehow, by supreme mental effort and determination, Andrés reached the end of his year as novice, still firm in his desire to be a priest.

Another fifteen days of spiritual exercise, complete silence, fasting, and prayer were spent just before he took the vows of his order. In these vows he promised to live a life of poverty, self-punishment, obedience, and celibacy.

After taking the vows, Andrés was a member of the order and could be called Padre Andrés, although another six years of study lay ahead of him before he could perform any of the rites of the church.

8

ORDAINED TO THE PRIESTHOOD

ANDRES stood in the middle of his small room, lost in thought. He had just finished packing his few belongings in preparation for moving on to another monastery, where six more years of study awaited him. During many dark hours of the past year the vestiges of his independent spirit seemed to have disappeared. He had learned to live one day at a time, following humbly the orders given by superiors, walking in strict obedience to all the many rules and regulations of the restricted life.

Standing in the room where he had endured so many hours of mental agony and conflict, he realized that some of his being was without feeling. The questions for which he had never found an answer were tucked away into the dark recesses of his mind. He had put every personal desire and ambition out of his heart and confessed every sin.

Although he had never achieved peace of mind, yet his mind was not in the upheaval it had been in previously. He had learned submission. There was one standard answer to every puzzling question: Rome was the final authority. To Rome God had entrusted the revelation of His will; Rome was infallible. Andrés no longer felt the impatience of his younger days. As he looked ahead, he realized that six more years was a long time, but it did not matter. He would accept what came, a day at a time.

"Are you ready to go?" Felipe asked as he passed Andrés's doorway. "The train is due in one hour."

"Yes, Felipe, all my things are packed," answered Andrés.

As usual, the young men went in a group to the station; but there was little opportunity for private conversation. In spite of semi-isolation, Andrés and Felipe felt a strong bond of friendship and understanding, and they had cherished it through the years.

As the train headed west again, the waste desert country was left behind. Andrés kept his face toward the window, drinking in the beauty of the green hills and charming valleys. Back in the mountains he had always loved, his spirit seemed to revive and he felt the thrill of familiar sights—the green carpet in the meadows, surrounded by stately trees. The cooler climate, as they gained altitude, was refreshing.

At their destination they found another ancient, moss-covered Franciscan monastery. So many years of his life had been spent in similar surroundings that Andrés soon felt a part of this new environment. It was a welcome change from the depressing desert country.

The days were occupied in religious activities and classes. The students who reached this monastery in their preparation for the priesthood were serious-minded young men who entered the heavy program with a will. Long hours were spent in intensively studying philosophy, theology, sociology, church doctrines, languages, politics, civil laws, and the Bible. When the Holy Scriptures were studied, one fact was always emphasized—Rome was the interpreter of what was read. They were told that the Bible was actually written for Rome's doctors of theology.

During his fifth year in this monastery, the political situation in Spain became critical. One morning the superior announced, "There appears to be a danger that even those studying in the seminaries will be drafted. It seems advisable that all students who do not want to go to war should plan to transfer to other countries."

Later that day Andrés discussed his future with the superior. "Padre Andrés, since your graduation is only seven months away, the faculty has voted to ordain you now and you may then finish your studies in Portugal. Your order has destined you to be a missionary in China. When your studies are completed, we will have plans ready for you to go to your field."

Andrés was filled with mixed emotions. To sail to a mission field halfway around the globe naturally appealed to him as an ambitious young man; but, on the other hand, he had looked forward to returning home and ministering in a village where he could be near his mother. It would be hard to tell her that he was leaving again and would not see her for many years.

The ordination was scheduled for a Sunday morning. Parents and friends were invited, but once again Andrés found himself alone on this significant day. Of the original class, only seven had come to the day of ordination.

After a short sermon by the archbishop, who had come

for this special service, the candidates formed a semicircle, prostrated themselves, and were covered with black cloths, signifying death to the world. Next, they rose to their knees and chanted in unison. The archbishop, after putting the oil of ordination on his hands, placed his hands on the heads of the young men kneeling before him, and one by one consecrated them to the priesthood. The priestly robes were then placed on them, along with various ornaments and medals. After their vows were repeated in unison, they participated in a mass. The archbishop led out, and the recently ordained candidates chanted the responses. Finally a sermonette was delivered by each young man.

After the service, the undergraduate students of the college congratulated and embraced their friends. There were tears as good friends came to the day of parting, and those who had finished their course realized that the long years of preparation were at an end.

Before leaving for Portugal, Andrés was given time to visit his people. On this occasion, too, he celebrated his first mass in his home village.

While María lived in the home of her cousins in the mountains grandmother grew weaker and finally died. Sad and lonely, María had felt that she had little reason to live, but hope returned and she began to plan a life for herself. One morning she said to her cousin, "Helena, I think it is time for me to go back home."

"But, María," the other woman protested, "you can't live alone. Your house may not even be standing."

"I feel that I must go. It is my home, you know. No

doubt some of my family have returned to their homes there by now. At least I must go and see."

"In that case, Cousin María, we will make the trip with you. Perhaps you will need the help of my husband to make your house livable again."

The following week the three journeyed on muleback over the mountains toward María's village.

"Look, there is my house! It is still standing!" María cried as she, Helena, and Mateo neared the old home.

"Yes," observed Mateo, "it's still standing. We will soon see if it is damaged."

Entering the yard, María hastened to the door. She had left the door barred, but now it was ajar and hanging crazily. Tears filled her eyes as she saw the chaos inside the house. Table and chairs were broken and bricks torn off from her stove and oven, and even the boards in the floor had been chopped up.

"Don't worry, María; we'll help you fix it again. At least the walls are standing, which can't be said of some of the houses in the village," Helena encouraged.

"Thank you, Helena; I'm so thankful you both came with me. It would have been hard to face this alone." María dried her tears and, with her cousins, began to plan how to restore order.

When repairs had been completed, Helena and Mateo returned home, and María picked up the threads of her former life. One day María made her way to the old church on the hill, where she found things in a sorry state. Images lay broken, while dust covered everything. The church had been without a priest during the troubled times, and the graveyard behind the church was neglected and overgrown with weeds. María spent many days restoring the church and the graveyard to their former well-kept appearance. Another priest came to the village, and once more the church on the hill was the center of religious activity.

One morning, when María went to the village to call for her mail, she found a letter from Andrés. Hastily tearing the envelope open, she read:

"DEAREST MOTHER,

"How happy I was to know that you are once again in our old home. I have dreamed and longed for the day when I, too, will be with you again. Because of the political situation, the day of my ordination has been advanced and I will finish my studies in Portugal.

"The ordination service will be a week from this next Sunday. It would be wonderful if you could come, but I dare not hope for that. I will be leaving for home the same day after the service to spend a few days with you. The superior here is arranging for me to conduct my first mass in our church there while I am home.

"The days will seem like years between now and then. When I think of coming home, I can scarcely contain myself. Until then, I remain as always,

"Your loving son,
"ANDRES."

As the realization dawned on María that she would soon see her son after an eleven-year absence, tears of happiness welled up in her eyes. One of the village women, whom María had known nearly all her life, noticing the tears, asked, "María, what has happened? Is there some bad news?"

"Oh, no, Doña Cristina, it is the best news I have ever had. Andrés will be here next week!"

"There, a little cry will do you good," said the older woman as she comforted the sobbing María.

The following days were filled with activity as María scrubbed and polished her humble home. The old Dutch oven, recently repaired, was kept hot baking the good things Andrés had always enjoyed as a boy. Everything possible was done to ensure him a joyous homecoming. Relatives and friends spent hours with María, checking details and plans for the few days that Andrés would be home.

When the young priest neared the village he noticed a group of people standing by the road. Coming closer, he was surprised to find that a large archway of flowers and boughs of trees had been constructed. His mother was among the group of villagers ready to welcome him.

"My boy, my boy!" cried the mother as she clung to his neck.

Many of the old friends of boyhood days were present, and it was a day of fiesta for everyone in the village. There was a feast and dancing in the street.

After the celebration, the villagers went to the church for a special service. Since it was the custom for a young priest to celebrate his first mass in his home church, everything had been arranged for the occasion.

The heart of Andrés was filled with emotion as he conducted the mass. María sat with a radiant smile on her face as she watched this self-possessed young man perform his duties with perfection. She could hardly realize he was the same boy she had sent away that day so long ago. According to her belief, Andrés's position as priest would ensure salvation to her household. When the service ended, the young priest sat in the confession box and heard confessions.

His days at home passed quickly. Although the days were filled by visits with relatives and friends, dinners, and festivities, Andrés found time to do some of the things he had dreamed of during the lonely years he had been away. He strolled through the village, across the old bridge, and up to the village mill. He smiled as he passed the Vásquez prune orchard, remembering the day he had made such a hasty descent from the tree and left behind the telltale jacket. He found time one day to climb the nearby hills where he had spent many carefree hours watching the sheep graze.

Andrés had not revealed his assignment as a missionary to China. María's happiness was complete, thinking she would not be parted from her son again. Somehow he could not bring himself to break the news to her, so he postponed it as long as possible.

On his last day at home, when the relatives had come to a dinner and fiesta in his honor, Andrés had a few moments alone with his mother.

"What is on your mind, son? Have you been keeping something from me?"

"It is nothing, mother. I guess it is just that I must go away again," he answered.

"But this time it will not be so far and you can come back often," María continued.

Knowing that the truth must eventually be told, Andrés said gently, "Mother, I may have to be far away for a long time."

"Andrés, tell me what you have been hiding! There must be something I don't know." María's voice was urgent.

"Well, mother, when I took my vows of the priesthood, obedience was one of the requirements. Since I have given my life to the church, I must go wherever I am sent."

"Of course, son, that is true. But it will surely be some-place in Spain, and you will be able to visit me occa-sionally," María added wistfully.

"I wish that were true," Andrés returned; "but it has been decided to send me as a missionary to China."

The shock of this revelation startled María, although she said nothing immediately. Andrés continued, "I have dreaded to tell you this, mother; but tomorrow I must go."

"Yes, you must go. The decision was made long ago," said the mother. "I should have known; but somehow, I had hoped—" María's head bowed in sorrow and sub-mission.

The news soon spread among the guests, and the rest of the day most of the conversation centered around the trip to China. For these people, many of whom had never even visited Madrid, China seemed to belong to another world, remote and unreal.

One of the young men among their guests had brought his guitar, and to his accompaniment songs of farewell were sung in Andrés's honor.

Andrés, who had always loved music, had composed a verse of farewell to express the pain and sadness in his heart. He sang while the young man strummed the chords on his guitar. These are the words, translated into English:

"Only with my heavy heart, I sadly leave.
I even saw the flowers in the garden weeping for me;
Weeping, yes, flowers for me, weep for me!
All the flowers, aye, wept for me!"

Andrés sang a second song he had composed in honor of his mother:

"Mother, to leave and cross the ocean
Causes my burning heart almost to break.
Unhappy fortune, from thee I have been parted;
Now will I see my poor mother no more.
If someday I return to my dear country,
If someday I return, tired of weeping,
Look on me, oh, mother, from the heavens,
For I will never cease to pray for thee."

The next morning Andrés gathered his belongings, and with his mother and a group of fifty friends and relatives, walked four miles to where he would catch his bus. The last, poignant moments Andrés spent with his mother, her arms around his neck and her face on his shoulder, would live ever in his memory!

9

INTO THE HEART
OF CHINA

THE seven months in Portugal passed quickly for Andrés. At the seminary he assiduously studied Portuguese, and in four months after his arrival he preached a sermon in Portuguese. After his examinations, Andrés was called to the office of one of his superiors.

"As you know, Andrés, the present political situation causes many problems. Two students who lack a year of finishing their course are in danger of being drafted. They, too, are to go to China. Therefore it has been decided to send them with you, under your care, to finish their training in the seminary there."

"If that is the wish of the superiors, then I shall do my best to help the young men," said Andrés, actually relieved to know that he would not have to make the long journey alone.

"You will proceed from here to France. There you will make arrangements for your long journey. There will no doubt be a delay of a few months, but you can use the time to advantage in learning French," the older man instructed.

Andrés felt a strange excitement, realizing that some of his dreams were to come true. The long, hard years of study and training were passed, and adventure lay ahead.

That same day, Andrés was introduced to the students who would be his companions on the journey. Pepe was a jolly fellow, his two hundred pounds giving him plenty of padding on all sides. The other young man, Francisco, was more serious, but friendly enough.

The three young men made preparations for the trip. They bade their friends good-by at Lisbon, where they boarded the boat for Bordeaux, France.

Standing on the deck and watching the shores of Portugal fade from view, Pepe said, "It is really a piece of luck to spend some time in France. I've always wanted to see Paris."

"From what I've heard, there are many interesting things to see in France," answered Andrés. "I have always longed to visit the famous village of Lourdes. It might even be possible to see a miracle take place while we are there."

"Do you think miracles actually take place there, Padre Andrés?" questioned Francisco.

"If the church gives credence to it, then it must be so," tactfully answered Andrés.

Arriving in Bordeaux, the young men visited a monastery of their order, where they found lodging. Andrés found a French grammer, which he kept with him constantly in an effort to learn the language rapidly.

"You are too ambitious, Andrés," commented Pepe one day.

However, Andrés had occasion to smile to himself in the weeks that followed. Pepe would come to him and say, "What are you doing today, Andrés? Would you have time to come with me? I can't make these Frenchmen understand me."

Before the date of sailing for China, the three young men visited Lourdes. As they strolled through the village, they were impressed with the many tourists. There were rows of shops with trinkets of all descriptions, said to have been blessed. Andrés was disappointed at the commercialism displayed everywhere. If this was a sacred place, it seemed sacrilegious to use it to make gain. He watched the sick who were brought to the water where the Virgin was said to have appeared, but he was disappointed when he saw no spectacular miracle.

In the evening there was a religious procession with an image carried from the church through the streets. Thousands of people followed, carrying lighted candles.

By midsummer Andrés secured passage for the three of them on a large ship carrying two thousand passengers. There was drinking, dancing, and merrymaking among the passengers, and the three clerics felt out of place wherever they went. Andrés took to spending a lot of time in his room, studying and reading. One morning, as they neared North Africa, Francisco and Pepe came running to the stateroom where Andrés was studying.

"Andrés, something terrible has happened. War has broken out. Our ship may not even be able to continue!" Pepe exclaimed, trying to catch his breath.

"War!" Andrés was truly alarmed. "Are you sure that the news is true?"

The three men, eager to know the latest news, joined the other passengers on deck. The passenger liner anchored in the Gulf of Aden to wait until safe passage could be assured. After dark, there were blackouts when not a light was allowed. Anxiety and tension gripped the passengers. Where, before, wine and dancing had been the order of the day, now rosaries and Bibles could be seen. Many Catholics sought Andrés, asking him to hear their confessions and pray for them.

"I don't like to refuse to listen to confessions," he told his companions; "but these people are only seeking religion from fear. The less I have to do with such persons, the better I will like it."

After a week in the bay, the ship got under way once more. It was announced that the vessel would be escorted by a warship.

Three months of travel ended for the three young men when they arrived in Hanoi and found lodging at a mission conducted by some priests of their order. Andrés struck up a friendship with a Padre Pablo and from him learned all he could about the customs of the Chinese. He was constantly amazed at the strange sights and sounds.

One day Pablo asked Andrés, "Wouldn't you and your friends like to visit one of our out missions? It will take only two or three hours in a car."

"Thank you, padre. It is what I have been anxious to do, for I would like to see some real Chinese life. I'm sure Pepe and Francisco will want to go with us."

On this trip the new arrivals saw many sights to attract their interest. They drove through miles of rice country, the swampy fields crowding the road on both sides.

"Look at those children climbing all over that water

buffalo!" exclaimed Pepe. "Isn't there danger that they will get hurt?"

"No," answered their host. "The buffaloes are very tame. The families who are fortunate enough to afford a buffalo to work their rice fields make pets of them."

"Please stop a minute, Pablo, I want to see the buffalo closer," Pepe asked, and then he climbed out of the car and walked down the road in front of it. As Pepe neared the children, he motioned that he would like to pet the water buffalo. But at that moment the buffalo began to snort and paw the ground. He turned and charged Pepe, who, in spite of his two hundred pounds, made remarkable speed toward the car. Running at full speed, with the snorting animal not far behind, Pepe passed the car and headed for a small tree a short distance away.

Since there was not sufficient room for the animal to pass, he pushed the small car off the road into the rice marsh. By the time he reached the tree, Pepe had climbed to the top branches and was looking down at him. The old buffalo pawed the ground and snorted; but, finding himself unable to reach the trembling Pepe, he turned and walked back to the children.

Pepe finally descended from his perch and returned to his friends who were struggling to get the car out of the mire. Pepe could not understand why his friends had been doubled up in gales of laughter.

"Pepe," Francisco remarked, "I never dreamed anything could make you move so fast. Since when did you become a professional tree climber?"

"You fellows might find you could run, too, if you had a mad buffalo after you," he commented dryly.

When they were once more on their way, Andrés asked Pablo, "Seriously, what happened to that buffalo? The children didn't seem afraid of him."

Pablo explained, "I'll have to admit that it was the first time I've ever seen a water buffalo really on a rampage. Evidently the old fellow thought Pepe was trying to steal one of the children, and he was going to the rescue."

"Well," added Pepe, "from now on I'll be content to view the creatures from a distance."

After a week at the mission in Hanoi, Andrés and his friends resumed their journey, this time by train. The French train that made the run to Kunming was comfortable, but its progress was slow and dangerous as it wound around treacherous mountain curves. Andrés shuddered when he looked down into gorges hundreds of feet deep.

In Kunming, the three travelers enjoyed the hospitality of the archbishop. Andrés was surprised to see priests with beards and simple Chinese dress instead of the customary robes. He understood the reason for this after he had endured a few days in the humid, hot climate.

While arranging for the trip into the interior, Andrés approached the archbishop. "Padre, can we get bicycles here?" he asked his superior. "I have been told that there is no train service from here on."

The older man laughed and answered, "I hardly think you would want bicycles. I'll arrange your transportation for you."

The morning of their departure for the interior of

China, Andrés called, "Are you almost ready, Pepe?" The "transportation" that the archbishop had promised was waiting outside the door in the form of three mules.

"I'm coming right now, Andrés, just as soon as this last bundle is tied," Pepe answered.

"Francisco and I have all our things ready to go," urged Andrés. "The rest of our group are congregating up the road and the order to start will be given any moment now."

Andrés, Francisco, and Pepe, mounted on their mules, joined the group with whom they were to make the journey. It was not considered safe for people to travel alone over the mountain roads because of bandits and wild beasts. There were more than sixty-five persons, most of them strangers to one another, in this party.

Twenty-five miles were covered the first day, and for Pepe, especially, the day was a torturing experience. Unaccustomed to horseback riding, he developed aches and pains early in the day. When the trail led over steep, narrow trails, he was frightened and at times dismounted and followed along on foot.

"I wonder what kind of hotel we will find in this place," Pepe commented as the caravan entered the main street of a small village. "I'll be thankful for a cold shower and a bed."

They came to a large thatch-roofed building, resembling a stable, with a courtyard.

"I suppose this is where the animals will be kept," Andrés remarked, noticing that the other travelers were dismounting and removing the packs from their animals. "I'll find out what the plan is for the night."

Handicapped by not knowing any of the Chinese language, Andrés could not speak to the Chinese guide. However, the priest found a young doctor and his bride who could speak French. "Dr. Wong, do you know where we are to spend the night?" he asked.

"Right here, padre. There is lots of room and you can select the spot you like and spread out your bed."

Andrés surveyed the dirty straw on the dirt floor and the medley of people and animals. "Is this the best place that can be found?" he asked.

"Yes," answered the doctor. "This is the place where travelers always stay. At least we will be safe from bandits and tigers."

Andrés slowly made his way back to his two companions, for he did not relish the reception he knew Pepe and Francisco would give to the plan for lodging.

"Well, boys, prepare yourselves; this is it. We are in the hotel where we will be spending the night."

"What do you mean, Andrés?"

"Let's not have any joking."

"This isn't a joke," said the priest. "We will have to make our beds here in this barn. I guess we will pioneer as true missionaries in China."

"If there is no other alternative, we might as well start preparing for the night," commented Francisco, the calm and practical one.

Andrés and his friends found a fire blazing in the center of the courtyard, with an immense pot of rice cooking over it. The three churchmen followed the example of their fellow travelers and accepted a clay cup and chopsticks. They dipped into the big pot of rice; but they soon found the chopsticks useless for them, so they took the easiest way and devoured the rice with their fingers.

They were given straw mats grimy with smoke and dirt. Someone casually informed them that the straw on the floor was changed every ten years, because of a religious superstition. Finding the most secluded corner possible, Andrés and his two charges lay down, weary and travel sore, to rest as best they could with bedbugs, lice, and fleas to molest them.

The caravan pushed on day after day, and those in the rear were tormented with the clouds of dust stirred up by those ahead. It seemed generally to be the lot of Andrés and his group to be near the end of the line, since Pepe had so many difficulties. The fat man was never comfortable in the saddle, and he couldn't walk fast enough to keep up with the travelers. One afternoon heavy clouds rolled up and a thundershower drenched the party. The mules became frightened and hard to manage; but they trudged on, for there was no place to stop for shelter. The three clerics were at the mercy of the elements, and they spent the rest of the day in damp clothes.

On the fourth day, as they were traveling through the brush, the Chinese guide shouted, "Lao fu!" Instantly, everyone became tense and nervous. Andrés soon learned that lao fu meant "tiger." The caravan halted, and everyone stood quietly peering into the bushes. Someone saw the tiger, but it disappeared in the thicket. However, the mules caught the scent of the wild beast and were frightened. It took some time to get the caravan reorganized and moving once more.

The trail became worse.

"Andrés, look at this trail. I simply can't go on. One misstep and a mule would go down hundreds of feet!" Pepe said with genuine terror in his voice.

"There is nothing else to do, Pepe. Don't be excited. Let your mule have his head, and keep on coming. You can't turn around here on this narrow trail, and you could not go back alone. You'll have to keep on."

The narrow trail led down the mountainside for miles until they reached the bank of the Yellow River.

"Do we have to cross that river?" Francisco asked, pointing to the stream that was several miles wide.

"You can see some of the primitive ferries rowed by natives," explained Andrés.

"But those rafts look so small and fragile. We aren't going on them, are we?" Pepe was alarmed.

"I guess we have no choice," Andrés answered. "There is no other way to get across."

When the last of the caravan had been transported to the other side of the river on ferries carrying twenty passengers, the travelers faced the prospect of climbing the steep trail to an elevation of five thousand feet. The path rose sharply from the river's bank, and it took much encouragement from the riders to urge the mules up the steep, slippery grade.

Only the fear of being left behind kept Pepe coming. He was sore in every muscle, and weak from dysentery which resulted from using contaminated water and food.

Weak and discouraged, he felt that he simply could not finish the journey; but Andrés and Francisco, also near exhaustion, constantly urged Pepe on.

Andrés and Francisco drove their mules over a steep, rocky place, and, looking back, shouted encouragement to Pepe. Pepe's mule, pawing at the slick rock to get a footing, lost his hold and fell backward.

"Francisco, look!" Andrés shouted. "Pepe's mule has fallen! Come quick! We must help him."

Andrés made his way down the treacherous grade to where Pepe and the mule lay. The priest noticed that the mule had fallen near the edge of the precipice. "Just wait, Pepe! I'm coming to help you. Are you hurt?"

"I don't know, Andrés. My back feels wrenched."

The two men were finally successful in getting the mule on his feet with the saddle and pack back in place, but nothing could induce Pepe to mount the animal.

Finding a level place on the trail, they stopped to rest, even though the caravan had gone ahead.

"Andrés, this is the end. I can see now that I was never cut out to be a missionary. I'm going back with the first caravan we meet going toward the coast. I'm returning to Spain."

"Pepe, you can't do that! We're over the worst of the road now." Andrés, touched by the tears that filled the eyes of his friend, continued: "Just think, Pepe, about Jesus who left heaven and came to this world to save us. China can't be any worse to us than this world was to Him. He was willing to suffer death. You must be willing to suffer for His sake."

Pepe looked back over the trail winding down to the great river. Finally he said with resignation, "I guess you're right, Andrés. We've taken a road from which there is no turning back. Let's get started again."

The three friends found the caravan resting on a grassy plain at the top of the mountain. The trail led down again, and when it became steep, Pepe was frightened, feeling sure that the saddle would slip down over the mule's head. But suddenly the cinch that held Andrés's saddle broke, and he found himself wrapped around the mule's neck, with his feet in the air. Andrés hung on for dear life until they came to a place where the mule could stop. Even Pepe could not resist laughing at the sight.

After twenty-five days of traveling, the group arrived at the mission station, where hospitality awaited them. The priest in charge led the mules to a stable and took the men to a bathhouse.

"Did you ever enjoy a shower so much in your life?" Pepe asked. "I feel like a new person."

A good meal awaited them in the dining room, and then the trio were shown to their rooms. They slept most of the time for the next two days.

"I'll have to stay now," Pepe confided to his friends, with a twinkle in his eye. "I wouldn't go back over that trail for anything."

10

MU YUIN HO

AFTER a period of rest, Francisco and Pepe went to the seminary, where they studied another year in order to complete their course. Andrés made his headquarters at the mission, where he found life taking on new meaning. He began the study of the Chinese language, eager for the day to come when he could go among the people as a real missionary.

The mission was ideally situated in a fertile valley surrounded by majestic mountains. A clear lake was within walking distance of the mission compound, and Andrés took many a stroll along the road leading to the water.

In six months Andrés was able to preach his first sermon in Chinese. He spent many arduous hours preparing and memorizing his talk.

"You did very well, young man, on your first sermon in Chinese. I was able to understand at least three words," an older missionary said, who came to congratulate him.

Andrés's face reddened. "Three words in a half-hour sermon," he thought to himself.

"But don't be discouraged, young man. When I preached my first sermon many years ago, the people were able to understand only two."

One day the missionary in charge of the mission said,

"Padre Andrés, it is time for you to find a Chinese name. Your Spanish name will be too difficult for the Chinese people to pronounce."

After discussing various names, he decided to take the name Mu Yuin Ho, which means "love, eternal peace."

After a year and a half the young priest was able to carry on a conversation in Chinese, and he traveled alone from place to place as an itinerant missionary, living in the manner of the people. Dressed in Chinese clothes, with straw sandals on his feet and a fifteen-pound pack on his back, Andrés went from village to village. His days of travel were arranged so that he would always arrive in a village before nightfall.

Andrés came to a country village where he was to spend a year in missionary work. Finding the church in a run-down condition, he set about repairing it, with the help of the local young people. Next he announced he would hold meetings in the church. The attendance was discouraging at times, but the enthusiasm of the young missionary never diminished. Each week he found more people coming to mass, and they also came to him with their problems.

One day a young man said, "Mu Yuin Ho, if you will pardon me, I have a question."

"Of course, young friend; what is bothering you?"

"You know, Mu Yuin Ho," he continued somewhat apologetically, "in the next village there is another mission, but it is not like your mission. There are no images on the walls, there are no candles burning, and there is no confessional. A man stands up and tells about a wonderful man named Jesus. He says that we need only to believe on this Man who came to the world many years ago and died that we might have salvation.

"We find your mission more like our Buddhist religion. We, too, have priests who wear robes, carry rosaries, and shave the tops of their heads. Our churches have idols, holy water, processions, and many other ceremonies. But this other mission is very different. The missionary teaches that a God far beyond the sky can hear and answer our petitions when we pray. The village people call your mission the religion of Mary, but they call this other mission the religion of Jesus."

Andrés was thoughtful and troubled, hardly knowing how to answer the sincere young man. The priest thought of the many doubts that had arisen in his own mind, especially during the year of novitiate.

"I suppose this other mission is doing a good work," he answered; "but, of course, there is only one true religion, that of Rome. Never forget that."

When the time came for Andrés to leave the little church and the friends he had made in the village, he was sad. Once more they would be left to carry on the best they could, little understanding the meaning of the religion that had separated them from the faith of their ancestors.

After a short rest at the mission headquarters, the priest went by train to the border of Tibet. Here he found another small church that needed reviving. He found many parallels between the heathen religion and his own. The temples were very much like the large cathedrals of Spain. There were heathen images with boxes in front of them where offerings could be made that would bring merit to the giver. There were also monasteries for monks and convents for nuns, and special days of religious significance, including a forty-day period similar to Lent.

After four years in the beautiful mountains of Tibet, Andrés was reluctant to leave, but orders came for him to go to central China. He found himself the village priest in a small community near Changtu. With untiring energy he built up the dying church, conducted classes for the young people, and celebrated the various saints' days, and festivals.

"Mu Yuin Ho, what do you think of people who can commune with the spirits?" one of his parishioners asked him.

"I think it is the product of someone's imagination," replied Andrés. "There probably isn't anything to it."

"I would like to take you up to a mountain village where there is a woman who is said to be possessed with spirits," persisted the parishioner.

"Let us go, then," Andrés answered quickly. "I would like to see this woman."

When the priest and his friend arrived at the village, they found the woman possessed of spirits out in her yard pounding rice. A baby was tied to her back. Bending over her work, she seemed not to notice the visitors as they entered the yard. They greeted her in her native tongue, but she refused to notice them. Andrés walked up to her and gently patted the baby. He was horrified to see that when he touched the baby the woman's eyes bugged out in a glassy stare. Waiting to be sure she wouldn't notice him, he again touched the baby ever so lightly. Once more the woman's eyes took on the same horrible stare. Satisfied that this was a demonstration of something beyond the human, Andrés hastily made his departure. He had little more to say to his companion about the incident.

In another two years Andrés was transferred to Peiping. On his journey he was accompanied by another priest, Padre Fernando. As the two men neared Shanghai, Padre Fernando became violently ill. He knew it was a gall bladder attack, for he had been ill before with the same symptoms. In Shanghai Fernando begged Andrés to help him find a doctor. They located a Catholic hospital and a doctor. But when the physician advised Fernando to have an operation immediately, he found that it would cost about a thousand dollars.

"I can't spend that much on an operation," he told Andrés. "I don't have any money, and I'm sure my order would never agree to that amount. Let's find another hospital. They say there are several in the city."

The two priests went from one hospital to another, only to hear the same story. Finally Andrés said, "Someone told me about another hospital; but it is a Protestant institution and we wouldn't want to go there."

"Why not?" asked the sick man, who by now was quite desperate. "I don't care what religion they have if they can help me."

Andrés accompanied his friend to the Protestant hospital, which was a Seventh-day Adventist institution. A kindly doctor examined Padre Fernando, and he, too, strongly advised an operation as the only possible cure.

"What will it cost me, doctor?" Fernando asked. "I find myself without resources."

"We are here to help people," the doctor began. "You are in missionary work, too. We will be glad to take care of you without any charge."

Fernando was speechless. With tears in his eyes, he said, "You will never know how much I appreciate this, doctor. You must be a real Christian."

Andrés, too, was surprised. He stayed in Shanghai to be with Fernando during his sickness, visiting him every day at the hospital.

One day during Fernando's convalescence, Andrés asked him, "What do you think of this place by now, Fernando?"

"It is wonderful, Andrés. I don't know too much about these people; but of one thing I am sure—they are real Christians. Before my operation, the doctor bowed his head and offered a prayer. Each evening a nurse comes to my bed and offers to say a prayer for me, before she turns out the light. A Mr. Lee, well versed in the Bible, visits me, and we have some interesting discussions." Mr. Lee came into Fernando's room once while Andrés was visiting, and he, too, was impressed with the sincere manner of this man.

Since Fernando was assigned to work in another town, Andrés left him when he had recuperated. The two priests continued writing, however, and Fernando's letters were full of news about Mr. Lee and the Adventist teachings he was learning.

Andrés found Peiping to be a city of charm and beauty. With sixteen universities, many beautiful gardens, and historic monuments, it proved to be a cultural center. While he worked there, a wave of communism spread from the north. At first there was no real alarm, for the people felt that the invaders would be driven back. However, as the threat continued, there was agitation, especially in the universities. Andrés was asked to speak against the invaders in some of the schools, and he did so with zeal.

Dangers increased until finally there was a great exodus of foreigners, but the priests and nuns stayed on. When the Spanish consul left, he asked his friend, the American consul, to help any Spanish citizens left behind.

One afternoon Andrés received a telephone call from the American consul. "I have information, Padre Andrés, that your name is listed with the communists as a war criminal. A plane is being prepared for the remaining missionaries from this section of the country, and I will see that you have passage on it."

"Thank you, Señor Consul," Andrés replied. "I am deeply grateful to you."

"Be prepared to leave at a moment's notice," the consul instructed.

The next day the consul called again, informing Andrés that the American legation's official car would be at his door early the following morning. The communists were only a few hours away. In the gray hours of dawn the priest made his escape in a ricksha, escorted by the consul's car. When it was necessary to pass sentries the consul informed them that the ricksha was in his party, and it was allowed to pass.

Escorted to a private airfield, Andrés found a plane already warming up its motors. There were about thirty persons, missionaries and religious workers of various faiths, ready to take off. When the plane was air-borne, the priest relaxed in his seat. He realized that his missionary work in China was at an end; he was sad to leave the people he had learned to love.

The plane had not been long in flight before the wings began to ice, and the pilot was unable to reach an airport. "Fasten your seat belts; no smoking," flashed the sign. The pilot spoke, "We are going to make an emergency landing."

Although there was no hysteria, the passengers waited, tense and breathless. Andrés noticed that the nuns and priests fingered their rosaries, while other missionaries held their Bibles and prayed. Expertly the pilot brought them down in an open field, and the ice was quickly scraped off the wings. Once again the plane took to the air, and this time it arrived safely in Shanghai.

On a plane from Hong Kong to Rome, Andrés found himself with seven Catholics and thirty-three Protestants. Heavy storms buffeted the craft as it flew over Indo-China and Burma, but it came through safely. There was a short stop in Calcutta for refueling, and another overnight stop in New Delhi.

Flying over the Holy Land proved to be a thrilling experience for Andrés. Although they made no stop, the pilot circled some places of special interest. One of the passengers, a Protestant minister, explained to the passengers the religious significance of some of the places. "There is the mountain where Abraham was called to take his son, Isaac, and offer him for a sacrifice; but at the crucial moment a voice from heaven told him that he had passed the test," the minister explained.

As the plane came in for a landing at the airport in Rome, Andrés felt the wheels touch the ground. Then with a new surge of power the plane shot into the sky again. A successful landing was made on the next attempt, and then the passengers learned that a boulder had been in the path of the plane. The pilot had gunned his motors just in time to miss it.

Andrés whispered to himself, "How thankful I am! God has been with me all the way from Peiping."

11

THE HILLS OF HOME

ANDRES went to a monastery in Rome belonging to his religious order. He was looking forward to meeting Felipe, his friend of seminary days.

"Andrés! What a surprise!" Felipe exclaimed when he saw Andrés standing at his door. "I thought you were in China."

"I was until a few days ago," Andrés replied, as the two old friends embraced.

"Come in, Andrés, and tell me what has happened to you." Felipe offered Andrés a chair in the simple room that was his home in the monastery.

"Let me catch my breath, old friend; there is so much to tell." Andrés sat back in his chair, taking a good look at his fellow priest. Felipe hadn't changed, he thought.

"You are thin, Andrés. Has life been hard in China?" Felipe questioned.

"I guess a missionary's life is never easy, Felipe, but I don't consider it a hardship. Perhaps the last few weeks have been strenuous. Since I was listed as a war criminal by the communists, perhaps I should consider myself lucky to be alive. By the way, what are you doing?"

"Right now I am teaching in one of the day schools. I rather like working with young people," Felipe answered.

Felipe was thrilled with the tales of missionary adventure that Andrés recounted. At last Felipe looked at his watch and said, "It's late, and you must be very tired. Tomorrow is another day. We'll do some sight-seeing. There are many interesting things you must see."

In the morning Andrés was eager to begin the tour of Rome. "The catacombs are one of the most interesting places, to my way of thinking," observed Felipe, as the two clerics left the old monastery. "Let's go there first."

While Felipe and Andrés followed a guide through the corridors of the ancient underground passageways, they talked of the early Christians who had lived in these secret places in order to preserve their faith in God.

"Tell me, señor," Andrés asked the guide, "where are the confessionals of these early Christians?"

"There were no confessionals," answered the guide. "The confessionals were instituted by the Roman Church many years later."

Andrés was surprised at this information. He had been taught that his religion was handed down directly from the time of the apostles; that Peter was the first pope. He tucked these fresh doubts in a corner of his mind, secretly planning to make an investigation of the history and origin of the confessionals as well as of some of the other practices of his church.

As the men wandered through the catacombs, Andrés felt that they were almost haunted by the spirits of the noble men and women who had sacrificed so much for what they believed. When he and Felipe started back to the monastery that afternoon, Andrés found himself trying to harmonize the picture of humble, earnest Chris-

tians hiding in dark tunnels and caves to preserve their
liberty of conscience, with the pompous ceremonies, elaborate churches, and intolerant attitudes of his church as
he knew it.

"Well, my friend," Felipe addressed Andrés a few days
later as he came into the room where the guest was staying, "we are fortunate. I was able to get tickets for an
audience with His Holiness tomorrow."

"Really!" exclaimed Andrés. "That really is good news.
I was afraid I might have to leave Rome without having
that privilege!"

The following morning, well in advance of the
appointed hour, Andrés and Felipe were in a palace waiting room with other visitors awaiting the arrival of the
pope. Andrés felt thrilled and excited as the time drew
near.

At last the moment came. The curtains were parted
and the royal chair, carrying a man who takes the place
of God for millions on earth, was carried in on the shoulders of palace guards. The chair was set on its pedestal,
and those who had come to see the pope went toward him
on their knees.

Andrés found himself humbly kissing the gold button
on the pope's shoe and remaining in that position until His
Highness gave him permission to arise. After receiving
the blessing, Andrés and Felipe walked silently from the
palace. On the street Andrés broke the silence. "He does
not look different from other men, does he?"

He delved into the recesses of his mind, resurrecting
some of the old doubts that had plagued him during his

seminary days. If only he could be sure that the pope was infallible. "How can a mere human be invested with the same powers as God? How can he make and change laws of conscience and forgive sins?" He almost wished he had not visited the palace, for the hour had aroused old doubts and upset his peace of mind. Something in his nature had rebelled as he knelt in front of the pope, waiting for permission to get to his feet.

Because of his long-standing friendship with Felipe, Andrés dared to ask him, "Have you ever doubted the divinity of the pope?"

"Yes," his friend replied. "I suppose most students of theology have at some time. However, I decided a long time ago that I believed more than I disbelieved. I know of nothing better. I guess there are some things you just have to take without proof. Those things don't seem to bother me any more."

Andrés decided that since he could never seem to find a solution, the best thing to do was to dismiss the problem from his mind.

Andrés said farewell to Felipe and traveled on to Spain. Riding on a train through the beautiful countryside near Barcelona, Andrés felt the thrill and exhilaration of coming home. So many things had happened since he had told his mother good-by ten years before. Back in the old, familiar surroundings of his native land, China seemed far away. He wondered how much his family had changed.

The last hour before reaching Barcelona seemed to drag. Nervously the priest looked at his watch and paced through the cars. When the train pulled into the station,

Andrés had his bag and was one of the first passengers off. He knew that no one would be there to meet him; still his eyes searched the crowd on the platform for a familiar face. Taxi drivers were vying with each other for business. Andrés selected one and settled himself in the seat.

"Where are you going, señor?" the plump, short driver, with a black, bushy mustache asked.

"Take me to the military air base," Andrés instructed.

Winding through traffic, they came to the office of the air base. Andrés inquired at the office for his brother. The girl at the desk found that Lieutenant Díaz was not on the base.

"Do you know where he lives?" he asked her.

"I don't have his exact address," she informed Andrés; "but he lives in the military colony. Perhaps you can inquire there for him."

Once more he instructed the driver, "To the military colony, please."

Arriving at the section of town that had been built to house the military personnel and their families, Andrés wondered where he would begin to look for his brother.

Seeing a man standing on the corner, he asked the driver to stop. "Would you happen to know where Lieutenant José Díaz lives?" the priest asked.

"No, I'm sorry," answered the stranger. "I've never heard that name."

The taxi driver turned around and asked, "Pardon me, señor, did you say Lieutenant José Díaz?"

"Yes, that is the man I am looking for," said Andrés.

"I'm so sorry I didn't know that before," said the driver. "I can take you right to his house."

"Really!" exclaimed Andrés. "This is a bit of luck. I never thought of asking you."

With mixed emotions Andrés looked intently at the house the driver pointed out as the home of his brother. There were two children playing on the sidewalk. "They must be José's children," he said to himself. "They are about the right age."

12

A ZEALOT IN COSTA RICA

WITH Andrés in China and José at military school, María had continued living in the old home; but life was lonely for her, and later, when José married and established his own home, she went to live with him and his wife. It is the custom in Spain for the parents or grandparents to be welcomed in the home of the younger generation. White hairs are honored and respected, and the counsel of the elders is not shunned. José's wife, Elena, was good to María. When little Victoria and Roberto were born, María was happy.

María always eagerly awaited the interesting letters from Andrés in China, for he wrote her in detail of his experiences and adventures.

"I'm really concerned over my brother in China," José confided to Elena one day, when no letter had come for many weeks. "I don't dare say anything to mamma, but stories are coming through of priests and missionaries being imprisoned and even killed. I wish we would hear from him."

"I hope nothing has happened to him," Elena replied, anxiety showing in her face.

One evening José came home from work in a state of excitement. "Mamma, Elena, there is news! Come and listen!" he shouted.

"What is it, José? Tell us quickly!" Elena urged.

"It is Andrés, my brother Andrés!"

"Andrés! Tell me what has happened to him!" María demanded in worried tones.

"It is nothing bad, mother. Someone who came in on a plane from Rome yesterday left a message for me. He said that my brother, Padre Andrés, had come with him to Rome and was stopping there. He will be arriving at Barcelona in a few days."

María covered her face and began to weep. Through the uncertain weeks without letters from her son, she had endured great anxiety.

"Andrés!" she cried. "I was afraid I would never see my boy again."

"There, there, mamma," José comforted. "This is a time for rejoicing, not weeping."

"I know, I know!" she said through her tears.

A week went by, and toward the end of the second week José and his family became anxious. "I don't understand why we have no word from him," José told Elena. "If something should happen to him now, I'm afraid mamma wouldn't live through it."

"He must have been delayed," Elena said reassuringly.

María and Elena were preparing the evening meal late one afternoon when Elena exclaimed, "There's a taxi in front of our house. I wonder who it is."

As she watched from the living room window she saw a man step from the taxi and walk up to the children who were playing on the sidewalk. He picked up Roberto and held him in his arms.

"Could this possibly be Andrés?" she thought. "I must find out before exciting mother."

Stepping out the door, she walked out to where the man stood talking to the children.

"Do we know you, señor?" she asked the stranger.

"Are you Elena, my brother's wife?" Andrés asked her.

"Then you are Andrés!" Elena cried. "I was sure when I saw your face. You are so much like José."

"Is my mother here?" asked Andrés.

"Of course; come in. She has been waiting for you ever since we got the message that you were coming."

They went into the house with the children following. "Mamma, mamma, there is someone to see you!" Elena called excitedly.

María came from the kitchen. "My son, Andrés!" With tears and a long embrace she welcomed her son. "So long I have waited for this day."

Joy reigned in José's house that evening. Elena scurried around the kitchen, preparing a cake, while María and José sat in the parlor plying Andrés with questions. Victoria and Roberto sat beside their uncle, listening to the stories. The priest was surprised to find that he enjoyed recounting the experiences that had seemed difficult when he went through them. The family was held spellbound by his account.

"Andrés, what will your next appointment be?" María ventured to ask one day, for she had feared the reply he might give. The days since Andrés's return had been happy ones and she was certain they could not last much longer.

"I haven't received definite word yet, mamma; but I am hoping that I will be in Spain for a while."

One Sunday Andrés was invited to preach and conduct mass in the church that María attended regularly. As her son stood behind the pulpit telling of mission life in China, the mother was touched by the emotion that stirred the audience. She felt repaid in a measure for the sacrifice she had made long years before when she saw her little boy go out of her life.

Andrés spent the next two years in Spain, preaching in various churches. Then the day came when Andrés received orders for his next appointment.

"It seems strange that you will be going back to the place where you were born," María said to Andrés after hearing the news.

"Tell me, mother, how I happened to be born in Costa Rica, in Central America." Andrés seldom spoke of anything involving his father, knowing that it was a subject that caused her pain.

"Well, son, when José was a baby, I went to Argentina to be with your father. Somehow he was born with a restless spirit, and he could not settle down. I found no security and no place to raise our family in the right way. There was nothing I could do but return to my home in Spain. We had relatives in Costa Rica and I visited there for a time on my way home. That is how you happened to be born there."

"Mamma, I have one great desire before I go again."

"What is it, son?" she questioned.

"When I was in China and thought of home, I always

thought of the village where I grew up. I could picture every inch of that village, and I looked forward to the day when I could walk down the streets again and look at those hills. Could we all go back there for a visit?"

"It's a wonderful idea, Andrés," María replied with enthusiasm. "I often long to go back myself. Your great-uncle and his family are using our house, and I know they will welcome us."

The weekend in the old home was a time long to be remembered. Andrés renewed old acquaintances and feasted his eyes on the scenes of his childhood.

When mother and son returned to the home of José, the priest was satisfied. His family went on the train with him to Madrid, where he boarded a plane for Central America. As he saw his mother waving to him, her silvery hair shining in the sunlight, he asked himself, "Will I see her again?" Then he said, "My life seems to be a series of farewells."

After a stopover on the island of Cuba, Andrés took another plane for Costa Rica. A priest representing his order met him at the San José airport.

"Padre Andrés?"

"Yes, I am Andrés Díaz," he replied.

"I am Santiago Rivera," his new friend informed him. "Can I help you with your things? There is a car waiting for us."

Andrés enjoyed the ride through the capital city of Costa Rica. As they drove to a small town in the country, he was amused to see the colorful oxcarts. They were painted in various bright colors, with elaborate designs.

He decided that the farmers must vie with one another to see who could have the most unusual and brilliant cart.

The countryside was luxuriant with tropical foliage. Andrés found that the climate was most pleasant. There was no oppressive heat such as he had endured in some parts of China, nor were the winters cold as in northern Spain.

"What is that place?" he asked Padre Santiago, as they passed a group of buildings where young people could be seen on the campus.

"That is one of the thorns in our flesh," Padre Santiago informed him. "That is the Colegio Adventista. It is Protestant, of course, and getting far too much attention around here. I don't know what they stand for, but they are winning too many converts. We need to find a way to stop them." Padre Santiago was plainly agitated over the matter.

When the priests arrived at the monastery, Andrés was given a room. He was to engage in missionary work in different parts of this small Central American country. Though Andrés had not been in Costa Rica long, he realized that his life here would be a pleasant contrast to the hardships of China. He could speak his own language, and the people had much in common with Spain.

Santiago was reading the daily newspaper one day when he exclaimed to Andrés, "Have you seen this? The Colegio Adventista has applied to the government for recognition as an accredited school. It is being considered by the Department of Education. Didn't I tell you that they needed watching?"

"Well, can't something be done to stop them?" asked Andrés.

"Of course, you have to be careful in dealing with the government," Santiago explained.

"It wouldn't be hard to stir up public sentiment. Then the people would put pressure on the government," Andrés suggested.

"If you think something can be done, why don't you make it your business to do it?" Santiago said, tactfully shifting the responsibility to Andrés.

Being a man of spirit and action, Andrés began to formulate plans to curtail the progress of the Colegio Adventista.

The director, who had labored hard to bring the school to government standards so that the graduates would have government recognition, was dismayed when he heard a speech on the radio by Padre Andrés. The priest called on all loyal Catholics to help prevent the hated Protestants from ruining the country with their schools and by proselytizing. This talk was followed by letters to the local paper written by Andrés. The question was discussed on the street corners and in the homes. Great was the disappointment of the faculty and students at the Adventist college when the campaign launched by Padre Andrés was successful in preventing the school from receiving accreditation.

Andrés was praised and applauded by his co-workers because of his success. In speaking of him, one of the superiors said, "Padre Andrés has fire in him. If you want something accomplished, put him at the head of it."

13

AS A PADRE
IN GUATEMALA

AS ANDRES left the monastery dining room and walked across the patio toward his room, Victoria, the servant girl, called to him, "Padre Andrés, here is your mail!"

Standing in the warm sunshine of the patio, the priest looked at each letter to determine who it was from. Noticing a long airmail envelope, his eyes widened in surprise. It was from the father superior, the one to whom he was directly responsible. Hurrying to his room, he laid the other letters on the table and hastily opened the envelope. After the first paragraph of formal greeting, he came to the real import of the letter.

"You will please arrange to finish your work in Costa Rica as soon as possible and prepare to go to the Republic of Guatemala. There you will receive further instructions as to your future responsibilities."

Andrés sank into the one hard, straight-backed chair in the room to collect his thoughts. He did not consider this to be bad news. To the contrary, in his lonely and somewhat monotonous life he sometimes welcomed a change. He hated to leave his friends in Costa Rica, the most beautiful country he had known; but he had heard, too, about Guatemala, the land of mountains, volcanoes, and earthquakes. It was known as the land of eternal spring. Yes, he looked forward to this new appointment.

When the giant Constellation taxied up to the modern airport in Guatemala, Andrés noticed the majestic mountains in the distance. The countryside was green and beautiful, the scenery picturesque. Emerging from the routine of customs inspection, Andrés saw that most of the passengers were greeted and embraced by loved ones and friends. With a pang of lonesomeness he realized that no one was expecting him. He took a taxi, giving the driver the address of the monastery. Settling back in the seat of the old limousine, he enjoyed the sights of the strange city.

At the side of the road he saw two barefoot Indian women and a small child, all dressed alike in large, shapeless blouses with tight wrap-around skirts. Both women balanced huge baskets on their heads, and had their arms filled with other things. They moved at a loping trot. Two oxen lumbered along, pulling a load of wood in a cart with wooden wheels. A barefoot man and boy walked in front of the load, the man prodding the oxen occasionally.

It seemed to Andrés that the streets were full of cars, motorcycles, bicycles, carts pulled by oxen, carts pulled by donkeys, and carts even pulled by men. The people were scurrying this way and that in a hurry to get someplace. The taxi pulled up to the curb in front of a white, imposing-looking building that occupied an entire city block. Andrés took his few pieces of luggage, paid the driver after a little discussion in which the driver attempted to overcharge him, and went through the double doorway of the monastery.

"I am Andrés Díaz from Costa Rica," he said to the priest he met near the door.

"Just a moment, please, while I call the superior."

Soon Andrés met the man who would be his superior while he worked in Guatemala. After greetings were exchanged, the older man, a bald, round-faced priest, said, "You will need to stay here in the capital a few days to arrange your residence papers, and then you can take a train to the coast. The village where you are going is not large, but there is a large population in the surrounding country. Since the church there has not been served by a priest for some time, I am afraid you may find things in bad shape. Do what you can for the church there."

Andrés recognized a challenge in the discouraging words, and he thought to himself, "If there is something to build up, I'll make the most of it."

In a few days Padre Andrés set out for his new parish. It was an all-day trip by train with a short bus ride to the isolated village where he was to make his home and carry on the work of the church. To his dismay Andrés found a run-down, deserted building, with only a few old women who might be considered faithful members. Among the other townspeople he sensed an indifference to the church.

Andrés found a room in an adobe building behind the church, which he appropriated for his own use. It didn't take him long to get settled. He swept and scrubbed the room, drove some nails on which to hang up his few clothes, and scouted around for a bed, table, and chair.

In spite of a dismal beginning, Andrés entered upon his new work with enthusiasm.

Osberto Córdova came home from his store one evening a few weeks later and said to his wife, "My dear, it looks as if this new padre is stirring up some dust around here. He already has a large class of children organized, and the town is full of talk about his doings. Perhaps we should start going to church again and find out what is going on. He really does seem like a sincere fellow."

"I'm glad to hear you say that, Osberto," his wife responded. "I'm afraid our children have almost forgotten what it is to go to confession."

Each Sunday found more and more of the people filling the chapel, until it seemed that the village life revolved around the once-forsaken church. Not only did the townsfolk appreciate the sermons that Padre Andrés gave on Sundays, but they came to him in times of trouble.

"I used to think that priests were more interested in the offering plate than anything else," remarked one of the members; "but this new padre seems to care about us. I've heard that he says masses free of charge to the poor."

In the midst of so much poverty, Andrés often felt conscience-stricken to charge anything for his services, and he put the fees below the usual amounts.

Some of the business people, realizing how much the new padre was doing without remuneration, became concerned for his material welfare. They noticed that some of his clothes were threadbare. It was, therefore, a pleasure for them to plan a surprise fiesta for their padre on his birthday. Hundreds of delicious tamales were prepared for the meal, and the townspeople came with presents for the padre who had won his way into their hearts.

As his congregation grew and he became better acquainted with the members under his care, Andrés found himself busy from morning till night. Many times he was called in the night to visit the sick or dying, and he walked many miles in all kinds of weather.

One evening, in the solitude of his room, he was pondering the problem, "How can I carry on alone here? Actually, there is enough work for several priests. I must devise some method to better organize my work."

He devised a plan that proved very successful. Selecting several young men whom he considered promising, he conducted a training class. In the class, Pedro seemed to stand out as a bright, willing, religious youth.

"Pedro, how would you like to give the sermon next Sunday morning?" Padre Andrés said to the young man one day.

"Oh, padre, I don't know if I could."

"If you need help in preparing your sermon, you can come to me. I would really like to see you try," Andrés urged.

After the sermon the following Sunday, the padre went to Pedro and gripped his hand. "I was proud of you, Pedro. You did a fine job. You are going to be my right-hand man."

One day when Pedro was visiting Padre Andrés, the priest asked him, "Will you be able to attend the Action Movement Congress? It will be three weeks from now."

"I haven't heard about it, Padre Andrés. What is it?"

"It is an organization in the church especially for the young people. The south coast of Guatemala is organized in one federation, and members meet in a central place once a year. I think you should go, Pedro."

"It sounds interesting, and I will certainly go if I can," the youth assured him.

When the day of the Action Movement meeting came, a group of young people, including Pedro, represented Andrés's church.

During the day there was an election of officers for the ensuing term, and it was a surprise to Andrés when his name was read as the new president. At this meeting a theme song was to be chosen from songs that had been submitted to the judges. Andrés, loving music, had written and submitted a chorus.

"Our new theme song has been written by the newly elected president, Padre Andrés Díaz," the judges announced.

Some months later Andrés was studying in his room when there was a knock on the door. Andrés was happily surprised to find Padre Sebastian, priest of a neighboring parish, accompanied by a friend he had met at the youth conference.

"Come in. It is good to see you again."

"I am going up to the Indian country at Momostenango," Sebastian said, "and I stopped by to see if you wouldn't like to go with me. They say it is an interesting trip."

"It is good of you to think of me, my friend. I can't give any reason why I shouldn't go." After a moment's hesitation, Andrés added, "Yes, I think I'll go. I'll be ready in a few minutes."

The men traveled in a jeep that Sebastian was driving. The road was rough, but after several hours of bumps, mudholes, dust, steep mountain grades, and some gorgeous scenery, they arrived at the primitive town of Momostenango. Surrounding the valley in which the town nestled were wooded hills with patches of green corn on the hillsides. Now and then a thatch-roofed hut could be seen, or the red, home-baked tiles of an adobe cottage. The road came down steeply into the village with cobblestone streets, and brightly dressed Indians were everywhere.

"Let's go to the church first and look up the padre. He can probably tell us what there is to see," Sebastian suggested, as the sturdy jeep wound through narrow streets. The village priest, Padre José, was friendly and gave the men a cordial welcome. While he visited in the churchyard, he offered Andrés and Sebastian cigarettes, but they did not smoke. Andrés had known other priests who smoked, and he realized that it was not prohibited; but somehow he felt it was not appropriate for a priest, and he had never taken up the habit.

Padre José suggested, "Wouldn't you like to see some things of interest here? There is the hill of the broken pots."

"Hill of the broken pots," repeated Andrés. "What could that be?"

As the three clerics walked up the hill, José explained some of the customs of the Indians. "The Indians here have never gotten away from their heathen beliefs; they are very superstitious. In fact, many of them are devil worshipers."

"I never expected to find devil worshipers in this country," commented Andrés, remembering the heathen practices he had seen in China.

"Tell us more about this hill of the broken pots," urged Sebastian.

"When someone dies, these people believe that they must attract the spirit away from the home where the dead person lived, otherwise it will hover around and haunt the family. They have a fiesta for all the friends and relatives. They take an earthen vessel that has been used by the deceased in his lifetime and carry it with great ceremony up to this hill. One of the native witch doctors performs incantations and breaks the vessel on top of the pile where thousands of others have been broken through the years. In that way the spirit of the dead is said to be released. Then the rest of the day is spent by the group in merrymaking, drinking, and feasting."

"Well, that is a queer custom," remarked Sebastian.

Andrés was silent, thinking in his own heart about the Catholic concept of the spirits of departed loved ones. After all, what kind of place was purgatory?

Andrés, Sebastian, and José stood on the hill looking at the mounds of broken pots, each busy with his own thoughts. In China Andrés had been plagued by the similarity between some of the rites and customs of Buddhism and those practiced by his own church. Again he found a similarity between the beliefs of these heathen people and those of his church.

Walking back to the village, Padre José spoke again of his people. "You see plenty of alcoholism here. These people drink like fish. On fiesta days you see them by the dozens go howling and swaying by your door. I often see a man and wife, both so drunk it is a question as to which one needs help the most. They eventually end up in a heap by the side of the road."

"You know, at one time I was afraid I might become an alcoholic myself," said Andrés. "It started with the wine of the Communion. I found myself drinking more and more on every possible occasion, until I became alarmed with myself and decided to take the situation in hand."

Sebastian had been listening to the other two men, but now added, "Well, in the solitary life we lead, I don't see anything wrong with a little drinking, as long as you keep yourself under control. I couldn't get along without it."

"I guess some people might say I'm somewhat of a winebibber myself," Padre José admitted. "It hasn't seemed to do me any damage."

As they rounded the corner they heard a bloodcurdling scream. Andrés and Sebastian jumped as though they had been shot. "Oh, don't be alarmed. That's just another drunk Indian," laughed Padre José. "The stuff they drink is almost straight alcohol."

Nearing the church, they saw people coming and going through the door. Those entering carried bunches of small candles and other small parcels. The three priests entered the building. When their eyes were accustomed to the darkness of the interior of the church, Andrés and Sebastian were astonished to see these people lighting the small candles and setting them on the floor of the church. The room had been cleared of benches with the exception of a few in the front. As the Indians lighted their candles, they scattered rose petals around and mumbled their prayers. A few "fortunate" ones had a pagan witch doctor with them to offer prayers. After the ceremony of burning the candles, they bowed to the various images of the saints along the walls of the church, and then they prayed to the Virgin Mary.

"Why are these people carrying on like this in a Catholic church?" Andrés asked in righteous indignation.

"Well, what can you do?" asked the local priest. "If you prohibit this, they won't come at all. After all, they still worship the Virgin and they still pay money into the church coffers."

Without saying more, Andrés went to one end of the room and began stamping through the burning candles, kicking them out as he went. He shouted at the poor, bewildered Indians to get their paganism out of the Catholic church. The Indians scattered, and before long the three priests were left alone in the smoke-filled sanctuary. Andrés was white and speechless, but he felt he had done a good deed. The other two priests shook their heads but made no comment. Later the three had a lengthy conversation concerning the work of the church in lands that are dominantly pagan. Andrés felt defeated when he realized that, to a large extent, the church had compromised with paganism.

Later Padre José had another suggestion. "There is a Protestant school here for the Indians that you might enjoy visiting. The director, a Señor Tahay, is a good friend of mine, even though we represent divergent religious views. I respect him as a man and for the work he is doing."

Andrés was surprised that Padre José had fraternized with Protestants, but he said nothing. It would be interesting to see how they operated.

"*Buenos días*, Señor Tahay," greeted Padre José as he met the little man with a big smile.

"Come in, Don José. I am glad you have come," Señor Tahay said warmly.

"I have brought some friends to meet you and to visit your school," Padre José explained. "This is Padre Andrés and Padre Sebastian."

"It gives me much pleasure to know you. Won't you come and sit down?" After showing his visitors to chairs in the patio, the director stepped into his living quarters to inform his wife that visitors had arrived.

When Señor Tahay rejoined the three priests, the local padre began to explain further. "I was telling my friends what you are doing for the Indians. They are interested in knowing more about your school."

"I shall be glad to answer your questions, gentlemen," the friendly director offered. "We are here to serve."

"What is the real purpose of your school?" Sebastian asked pointedly.

"The real purpose of our school," Señor Tahay replied, choosing his words carefully, "is to help these people know the Christ who died for them, and to find a better way of life. As you know, the future of any people is in its youth. If these young people can be taught the Christian way, their homes will be built on different principles."

"Do they still hold to their heathen practices when they join your mission?" Andrés questioned.

"No, there can be no fellowship between Christianity and heathenism. As you know, one is from God and the other is from the evil one. The young people who come here must drop their pagan ways and change their way of life. We teach them healthful living, cleanliness, and other practical things."

"Tell them about the industries in the school," interrupted Padre José.

"We feel that every young person should know a trade. Such training will help them overcome the poverty of the community. We have several industries by which the students may earn part of their expenses. There is furniture making. The chairs you are sitting on were made by the students. The beds and mattresses in the dormitories were made by them. The girls learn cooking and sewing, and we are now beginning a blanket industry."

While the three priests sat listening to the director, the bell rang and classes were dismissed. The group of young people emerging from the classrooms presented a striking contrast to the people they had seen on the streets. They were clean and neatly dressed, and their faces were shining.

At this moment the director's wife came with a tray of cold lemonade. Señor Tahay introduced her to his visitors, and she extended a welcome to each one.

"My wife is very busy," the director explained, as the woman left the patio. "She oversees the meals and has charge of other activities in the school."

"We won't take more of your time today," Padre José said, rising from his chair. "Thank you so much, my friend, for your kindness."

"We are glad to have met you and to know more about your school," Andrés declared as he shook hands with Señor Tahay.

Walking back to their car, Andrés confided to his friends, "I've had a low opinion of Protestants, but actually that man seems very sincere and good. What did you say the name of his mission is?"

"He belongs to the Misión Adventista," informed Padre José.

"Adventista! Why, that is the same name as a school in Costa Rica."

Andrés said no more, but many questions crowded into his mind. Had his actions in Costa Rica against the Colegio Adventista been justified?

14

A TROUBLED MIND

AFTER preparing his own food in his room for a few months, Andrés made arrangements with the Córdova family to board in their home. They had become good friends, and Osberto and his wife were loyal supporters of the church.

"Have you met our friend, Señora Gonzales?" Osberto asked Andrés one evening when they were celebrating one of the children's birthdays.

"No, I have not had the pleasure," Padre Andrés answered.

When Andrés was introduced to Señora Gonzales, he realized that she had never been to any of the services at his church. When the priest found an opportunity later in the evening, he inquired as to her church affiliation.

"I belong to the little church on the other side of town," she informed him.

Andrés had not thought of another church in the town, but now he remembered a small building in the district she described.

"We have our services on Saturday, which the Bible calls 'the Sabbath,'" she continued.

"What is your church called?" Andrés questioned.

"It is the Adventistas del Séptimo Día," she answered without hesitation.

Noticing that others at the party were looking at him as he engaged in conversation with this Protestant woman, Andrés did not discuss the subject further. Later that week, however, Andrés was surprised when he answered a knock on his door to see Señora Gonzales, whom he had met at the birthday party.

"I don't want to bother you, Señor Díaz. But after thinking over the questions you asked the other night, I thought I would bring you this magazine. It will give you a good idea of what I believe." As she handed him the magazine, *El Centinela,* she smiled and left.

Andrés took the periodical and thanked her, thinking he would destroy it at the first opportunity. However, as he leafed through it, an article caught his eye. He sat down and read the article about Christ's second coming. Before destroying the paper, he had read it from cover to cover.

A short time after reading *El Centinela,* Andrés again happened to meet Señora Gonzales at the Córdova home. This time she was accompanied by her mother, an elderly woman, named Señora Martínez, whom he found to be an interesting person.

During their conversation he was surprised when the kindly woman said, "Señor Díaz, you seem to be such a sincere man. What a pity you are in the wrong church and will be lost!"

Andrés's face flushed, and he asked, "What makes you think that I will be lost?"

"My Bible says that those who keep the commandments of God will be saved," she answered boldly.

"And which commandment do you imagine that I am

not keeping?" Andrés countered, secretly suspecting that some gossiping old woman of the town had been manufacturing scandal about him.

"Why don't we open the Bible and read the commandments, and you can see for yourself, Señor Díaz?"

Andrés asked to be excused to go to his room and bring his own Bible. The older woman readily accepted his Catholic Bible, and she turned to the twentieth chapter of Exodus.

After reading the second commandment, she stopped and said, "Here is one commandment that you are breaking. Don't you see that we are forbidden to make a graven thing, let alone bow down and worship it?"

Andrés didn't answer for a moment. In his own mind he felt this was a hard question to answer. "Of course, señora, you realize that we don't really worship images. We worship the thing that they represent."

Without pressing the matter further, Señora Martínez went on. When she came to the fourth commandment she read it slowly and clearly. Then, looking at the young priest, she said, "There is the other one, Señor Díaz."

Andrés read the fourth commandment again. He was puzzled. How could it be that he had never noticed that word "seventh" before? Groping for something to say, he offered the lame suggestion that we could begin our week on Monday, thus making Sunday fall on the seventh day. But Señora Martínez was quick to point to the calendar hanging on the wall, calling his attention to the fact that the first day of the week is Sunday and the seventh is Saturday.

Finally Andrés told the woman, "If you will pardon me, señora, these things have never been brought to my attention before. I will need some time to study them before answering your questions. I'm sure there is an answer."

"I have some excellent reading material that will throw light on this subject, Señor Díaz. I will see that you get it," Señora Martínez assured him.

In the quiet of his room Andrés took his Bible and turned to the twentieth chapter of Exodus and reread the Ten Commandments. He had been troubled for years about the images in the churches. He knew that the majority of the people did worship the wooden image they were kneeling before. He had always had to silence the questioning in his mind with the thought that it was a doctrine of divine authority given by the pope. But now the thought persisted, "Why should the teachings of the church contradict the teachings of the Bible?"

As far as the seventh-day Sabbath was concerned, this was something new to him. He decided that, to satisfy his own mind, he would study the whole subject for himself. He began that evening to read the history of the church from the days of the apostles to find out how the first day came to be the day of rest.

After days of careful study, he found that there is no record of the apostles having kept sacred the first day of the week. Moreover, he found that Sundaykeeping did not officially come into the Christian church until the fourth century, when, at the Council of Laodicea, the attempt was made by vote to transfer the sacredness of the Sabbath from the seventh to the first day of the week.

Before leaving the town for her own village, Señora Martínez stopped by the priest's room. "I have two books that I would like to lend you, Señor Díaz. I believe you are an honest man. I want you to read and evaluate them." She left *Steps to Christ* and *The Great Controversy*.

That night Andrés found himself so interested in the smaller book, *Steps to Christ*, that he read it through before he retired.

"This is a wonderful book," he admitted aloud. "There is nothing objectionable about it. In fact, I believe I will build a sermon from the chapter on faith."

In the months that followed, Andrés found himself turning again and again to the little book for inspiration and spiritual strength. The thoughts for many of his sermons were gathered from its pages. As for the other book, *The Great Controversy*, he devoured every word of it. He was thrilled with the story of the early Christian martyrs, and of the Waldenses in the mountains. He rebelled at first when the fallacies and mistakes of his church were discussed. However, he was willing to read on, and he gained a new concept of how the eternal principles of the Christian faith had been preserved down through the years. Most of his reading was done in the late hours of the night so that no one would discover him reading Protestant books. When not in use, the books were hidden in the bottom of his trunk.

When Andrés had finished the last page of *The Great Controversy*, he found himself in a dilemma. He had not entirely lost his faith in the Church of Rome, but now he had grave doubts. The conflict was great, but his sincere desire for truth rose above his background and training. He was convinced that the seventh day was the Sabbath of the Bible, and that Jesus and the apostles had known and kept no other day. It seemed that the spark left the priest's work, and he went about his church duties in a mechanical way. He said masses for the dead and dying; he listened to confessions. He even had a procession at Easter, when the images of Mary and Christ were decorated and carried on the shoulders of men through the streets to the somber sway and rhythm of a band playing solemn music. His parishioners paid their fees for the privilege of carrying the images or wearing the costumes in the procession. Yet Andrés could see sham in much of his activity. The longer and deeper he studied, the more he was haunted by a fear that, after all, the Church of Rome was not infallible. The belief in the infallibility of the church had been reinforced in his mind again and again at the seminary; but now he doubted the doctrine. He came to believe that the pope was another mortal being, who would have to depend on the blood of Christ for his own salvation.

In her home, Señora Martínez had not forgotten Andrés. She told her husband about the conversation she had had with the priest. "Somehow I have the feeling that he is an honest man. I believe he will read the books I left him."

"We must pray earnestly for him," her husband answered. "Let us pray every day that God will show him what is truth."

"I believe that I will send him a card to enroll in the

Voice of Prophecy correspondence lessons," Señora Martínez added. "It will do no harm, and there is just a chance that he might study them."

The following day she mailed Andrés more literature, along with the enrollment card to the Voice of Prophecy free Bible course. Andrés was secretly grateful when the package arrived. After deciding to have the Bible course come to him under a fictitious name, he mailed the card in and waited for the first lesson.

Studying the Bible in a systematic way proved to be a wonderful experience for Andrés, and he delved into each lesson with enthusiasm. Andrés was convinced that the seventh-day Sabbath was binding upon Christians. As to how he could keep it, he did not yet know. He was also convinced that Ellen G. White had been inspired of God to write her messages.

One day Padre Andrés had occasion to visit an elderly priest in a nearby town. While they were visiting, there was a knock and the old priest opened the door to find a poorly dressed old woman.

"Padrecito, my husband died last night. I want you to come and say a mass for him." Her eyes were full of tears as she added, "How can I be sure he will be taken to heaven? He was always so good to us; he was a good man."

The old padre, eyeing her closely, answered, "Yes, señora, I will come. Which mass did you want me to say for him?"

"I don't know what you mean, padre. Are not the masses that you say for the dead all the same?"

"Oh, no," said the priest. "There are three classes, or

kinds, of masses: first class, second class, and third class."

The old woman questioned further, "What is the difference?"

Then, to the astonishment of Andrés, who had heard every word, the old padre answered, "Well, señora, there is a great difference. The first-class mass will take your husband out of purgatory where he is now and put him safely in heaven. Then you will never have to worry about him again. That will cost you $100." Ignoring the shocked expression on the old woman's face, he continued, "The second-class mass is not quite as good, because it does not require as much sacrifice. It will take your husband out of purgatory only from his waist up. This will cost $50. The third-class mass will take him out of purgatory only from the top of his head to his mouth. That one costs $25. "

The old woman turned away dejectedly. "I am just a poor woman, padre," she said. "I have no money, but I will never be able to sleep well when I think of my poor husband suffering in purgatory. I will have to go and try to borrow the money. When I get enough I will come back. Good-by until later, padre."

When he turned back to Andrés after watching the old woman hobble away, the old priest wore a self-satisfied expression. He seemed irritated when Andrés spoke up, "Padre, how could you do such a thing?"

Surprised, the older man said, "Do what? What do you mean?"

"How could you deceive that poor old soul? Couldn't you see that she is half-starved? How could you expect her to pay even $25? That business about getting her husband out of purgatory just to his mouth is a lot of nonsense." Andrés was vehement.

"Well, young man," the old priest countered, "if you don't look out for yourself in this world, no one else will. That's plain business."

Andrés was shocked. Before dismissing the subject, he added, "I'm afraid if that is what it takes to get along in this world, I'll always be poor. When I charge for masses, I take into consideration the circumstances of the people."

Such experiences with his fellow priests served only to confuse Andrés the more and to raise again the doubts that had lurked in his mind concerning the practices of the Roman Church. How could people believe that such practices had any relationship to the teachings of the meek and lowly Jesus? According to the Roman Catholic system, the more wealth you had, the more certain you could be of gaining heaven. Andrés remembered that Jesus said it was easier for a camel to go through the eye of a needle than for a rich man to enter heaven. In the last few weeks he had read his Bible more than ever before in his life, and he was seeing the vivid contrast between the religion of Christ and the apostles and the traditions of the church to which he had given his life. Nowhere in Christ's teaching did he find the sanction of a cold, formal worship; and the Master did not charge for His ministry. The Gospels told of Christ's life of poverty and of His unselfish love and ministry, with never a mention of any kind of remuneration.

Returning to his home that day, Andrés resolved that he would continue to study his Bible, comparing the truths he found with the teachings of the Roman Church. Somehow he must know and be satisfied that he was following his Lord.

Andrés was startled one morning by a rap on the door. To his surprise, at the door stood two of the women whom he recognized to be Protestants. He greeted them, and after some small conversation, one of the women tactfully informed him that they were Seventh-day Adventists. "We have an Ingathering campaign every year to help support our world-wide mission work," she explained. "There are schools and hospitals, leper colonies, and clinics for the poor. I'm sure you recognize that this is a worthy work."

"Of course, señora. In fact, I have been in China and have seen what the missionaries are doing. I will be glad to donate." Andrés thought of his experience in Shanghai with Padre Fernando. He gave the women five dollars, and went into an adjoining room where a visiting priest was staying and invited his friend to donate to this worthy cause. The other priest shook his head, but a queer look crossed his face.

As the weeks passed, Andrés found it more difficult and uncomfortable to carry on his church work. He found great satisfaction in ministering to the needs of his congregation, and his heart went out to those in trouble or sorrow; but he struggled between belief in the Bible teachings and church tradition when he said mass, listened to confessions, or honored the various saints.

"I must do something to get things settled in my mind," he told himself. "If only I could talk this over with some-one, someone who could answer my questions. There is no one here that I dare to confide in. If only I could talk to an Adventist minister."

The solution to his problem came sooner than he had expected. When he was in the post office one day he met one of the women who had solicited him for funds. They exchanged greetings, and she asked if he had read the literature they had given him.

He avoided her question, but with courage he asked, "Señora, who is your bishop?"

She smiled and answered, "Señor Díaz, we don't have a bishop. But we do have a man, an American, who is the president of all of our churches in Guatemala. Of course, we have many local pastors, too."

Andrés was eager. "This American, where does he live?"

"Well," replied the woman, "our mission office is in Guatemala City. You would find him there."

Andrés asked further, "Did you say he is an American? Can he talk Spanish?"

Andrés had studied a little English, but he was not able to carry on a fluent conversation.

"Oh, yes, Pastor Lawson speaks good Spanish. He always preaches to us in our own language."

"One more question, señora," Andrés went on. "I noticed that you called this man 'pastor.' What is the reason for that?"

"We believe that the term 'father,' used in a religious

sense, should be reserved for God the Father. In fact, there is a verse in the Bible which instructs us to 'call no man father.' I suppose the term pastor is used because ministers are to care for the flock."

After obtaining the address of the mission office, Padre Andrés went back to his room and made plans to visit the capital. He was anxious for an interview with Pastor Lawson.

15

THE PRIEST GOES
VISITING

IT WAS a typical day in the life of missionary Lawson. After breakfast and worship with his family, he drove the jeep station wagon through the iron gate that kept intruders out and the children inside the yard of the modest home.

Marina, the girl who helped his wife in the house, padlocked the gate again, after calling one of their large dogs back into the yard. It seemed wise to keep dogs in the city, especially after the revolution, for there had been an outbreak of crime and violence. Pastor Lawson felt that the dogs were some protection for his family when he was gone on long trips to visit the churches.

As he drove down the busy street of Guatemala City, dodging carts and stray pedestrians who insisted on walking in the street, his thoughts were running ahead to the different activities and problems that awaited him in the office. He slowed down for a herd of goats that was driven by a boy, who stopped at a house when people brought out a pot or pan to purchase fresh milk. The boy would milk one of the goats, using the container the customer furnished.

The office workers, ministers, and stenographers gathered with Pastor Lawson in his office for morning worship. Many times special problems were made a subject of prayer. Always God's care was petitioned for every minister, literature evangelist, and teacher. They didn't forget the faithful laymen who gave unstintingly of their time to win others to Christ.

Two colporteurs were in the outer office waiting to see Pastor Lawson when he came from the worship hour. He greeted them warmly, "How are you, Pedro? It is good to see you. How are the books selling? I noticed you had a good report last month."

"Yes, pastor, the Lord did bless me last month; but I have a little problem," the colporteur answered. The mission president discussed the problem and helped Pedro find a solution to it.

After two or three other interviews, Pastor Lawson said to María, his secretary, "I am going to the palace on this problem of our schools. If anyone wants to see me, tell them I'll be back at two o'clock."

Pastor Lawson had been gone only a short time when Raquel, the secretary who acted as receptionist in the outer office, looked up and saw a man with a clerical collar.

"What could bring a priest to the mission office?" she asked herself, half-frightened.

"May I speak with Pastor Lawson, señorita?" the visitor asked.

"I'm sorry, señor, Pastor Lawson left a few minutes ago. We expect him back this afternoon at two o'clock," Raquel answered.

The priest, who was none other than Padre Andrés, was

visibly disappointed. Apparently undecided as to what his next move should be, he hesitated before saying, "Very well, then, I shall leave the address where I can be found in this city. Will you please ask him to call on me at his earliest convenience?"

"Of course, señor, I will give your message to Pastor Lawson," the secretary assured.

After he had gone, Raquel hurried into the other offices to tell the secretaries about the visitor. "Do you suppose he has come here to make trouble?" she said to María, who was Pastor Lawson's secretary.

"I never heard of a priest setting foot on 'heretic' soil before," said one secretary. "I wish Pastor Lawson had been here."

When the president arrived at the office shortly before two o'clock, Raquel said, "Pastor, we had an unusual visitor this morning. A priest came here, looking for you."

"A priest! Are you sure?" replied the astonished American.

"Oh, yes, pastor, I am sure. He left his name and address, and asked that you call on him." Raquel handed him the card the priest had left.

"Well," mused the missionary, "one never knows what to expect. This is a new one. I believe I will see him at once."

Pastor Lawson located the street mentioned on the slip of paper and began looking for the number. Finally he discovered that the number he was looking for was above the door of a large Catholic church.

"Surely he wouldn't ask me to come to the church to

see him," the missionary thought. "Could this be a trick?"

He hesitated at the door for a moment. He inquired of the first person he met for "Padre Andrés Díaz," the name on the slip of paper. The young man said he would call the padre.

As Pastor Lawson stood waiting, he looked around him. "What a gorgeous church!" he said, half-aloud. There were ornate carvings and beautifully ornamented, life-size images. There were ceiling-to-floor panels of rich lace draperies. The furniture and paintings were tastefully selected. A hushed atmosphere pervaded the sanctuary, as a worshiper now and then slipped in and knelt in a pew or before one of the images. "What an effect all of this solemnity and beauty must have on the minds of those who worship here," thought the missionary. "Many of the members have only mud floors in their homes."

He had stood in the poorer section of the city cemetery, and watched a family lower a loved one into the ground without benefit of clergy, without a song or prayer, because they were unable to pay the fee.

His thoughts were brought to a halt when a man about his own age stood before him. Pastor Lawson was impressed with the honest, clean-cut face.

"Señor Lawson?" the young priest asked, extending his hand.

"Yes; are you Andrés Díaz?"

"Thank you for coming, Señor Lawson. I have been very anxious to meet you," the priest said eagerly.

"I am glad if I can be of service," returned the mission president.

After looking around to be sure that no one was listening, Andrés explained in a soft voice, "Someone gave me several Adventist books. I have read them and now I have many questions in my mind. I was told that you could help me."

"This is interesting," thought Pastor Lawson. Aloud he said, "I will be glad to do anything I can, Señor Díaz. Wouldn't it be well for you to come to my office where we can talk in privacy? This is a very public place."

"You are right," replied Andrés, breathing easier. "I will meet you there in a little while."

Behind the closed door in Pastor Lawson's office, the priest and the missionary began their conversation.

"I am curious, Señor Díaz, to know how you became interested in these things. You must know this is very unusual," said the president.

"Yes, I suppose it is," Andrés answered. "Actually, it started one evening when I met a lady from your church who was visiting in the home of some of my members. Her name is Señora Gonzales. Do you know her?"

"I most certainly do. What happened?"

"This Señora Gonzales brought me a magazine, *El Centinela*, which I enjoyed reading. Later I met her mother, Señora Martínez, and she really set me to thinking. She said I wasn't keeping the Ten Commandments. Naturally I was taken off my guard and insisted on knowing which commandment I wasn't observing. She read them to me and pointed out that I was breaking both the second and fourth commandments and teaching others to do the same. I've always tried to do God's will and be honest in my religion. I had to get things straightened out in my mind, but the more I studied, the more confused I became."

The two men launched into a discussion of the main Adventist doctrines. Pastor Lawson was surprised to find that the priest believed he should keep the Sabbath, and that he also was convinced that Ellen G. White was inspired of God. However, concerning man's state in death, the priest was still greatly puzzled. He could not understand how a man lost consciousness in the sleep of death. Although Pastor Lawson read many texts from the Bible, showing that the dead are asleep and that they "know not anything," Andrés could not grasp this new doctrine.

"If you are honest with God, my friend, and pray for understanding, His Spirit will illuminate your mind with the truths from His word. Keep studying and praying," Pastor Lawson counseled.

"Please pray for me, Pastor Lawson. I must find peace of mind. My most earnest desire is that God will show me the truth. I cannot possibly imagine any course apart from the priesthood, to which I dedicated my life in childhood. In fact, to think of leaving it fills me with dread and fear; but God knows my heart. My sincere desire is to follow where He leads." An expression of tension and worry was written on the priest's face as he spoke.

"God's love for His children is beyond our comprehension. If you put your trust in Him, pray for divine guidance each day, and seek wisdom to understand His word, you need not fear. You will take only one step at a time."

After a short prayer, Andrés and Pastor Lawson gripped each other's hands. Selecting some books from his library, the missionary handed them to the priest, saying, "Perhaps these will be of some help to you as you study further. Remember, we are ready to help you in any way we can. We'll be praying for you."

On the following morning, the Sabbath, Andrés had an intense desire to visit the church of the Adventists. After his morning devotions at the Guatemala City Catholic church, he walked to the simple Adventist chapel, which adjoined the office where he had visited the mission president the day before. As he neared his destination, he was fearful of being seen. He walked more slowly, looking to the right and the left, and hoped no one recognized him as he entered the church.

Someone was teaching the Sabbath school lesson. Andrés didn't understand the procedure, but a friendly young man stepped to the back of the room where the visitor was standing and explained each part of the service to him. Andrés was impressed, for it reminded him of the methods used in the early apostolic church. There was no monotonous repetition of meaningless phrases. Instead, there was an atmosphere of devotion and dedication in the study of God's word. The young people seemed to know the answers to various questions concerning the Scriptures.

It was a mild sensation in the church on Second Avenue in Guatemala City that day to have a priest visit the service. Those who chanced to look around and notice the clerical collar that Andrés wore nudged their neighbors. "What could bring a priest inside a Protestant church?"

was the question in the minds of the people. Many offered silent prayers that nothing would be said or done to leave a wrong impression in the mind of the visitor.

"Wouldn't you like to sit down?" the tall young man invited.

"No, thank you, I think I would rather stay here," Andrés answered, feeling more inconspicuous at the back of the sanctuary.

The young man stayed beside him throughout the service, answering his questions, sharing his hymnbook, and doing all he could to make the priest feel at home. When the offering plate was passed, some members were surprised to see the visitor place a dollar on the plate. During the congregational singing, he also joined in the hymns.

"I have a strange feeling," Andrés thought. "I feel as though I were in a meeting of the early Christians in the days of the apostles. I feel that these people are real Christians, not heretics as I've always thought."

Mrs. Lawson, the pastor's wife, with her children, sat in the front pew near the piano. Her husband was visiting another church that morning; but he had told her of his thrilling visit with the priest. When she saw the priest standing near the door, she was sure it must be Andrés Díaz.

At the close of the service Mrs. Lawson hurried to the rear of the church, where some of the young people had already engaged him in conversation. She welcomed Padre Andrés. "We are so glad to have you here this morning, Señor Díaz. I am Mrs. Lawson. My husband told me of your visit yesterday."

"Oh, you are Pastor Lawson's wife. I am very happy to know you."

"Did you enjoy the service?"

"Very much, señora. It has been a wonderful experience. Where is Pastor Lawson?" Andrés was disappointed not to see his new friend at the service.

"He spoke in Escuintla this morning. I know he will be sorry to have missed you. Will you be back again?" Mrs. Lawson asked.

"No, I must leave the city this afternoon." Then Andrés added earnestly, "Please pray for me. I am having a real struggle."

The missionary's wife was quick to reply, "Our family and all of the church members will be praying for you. May God bless and guide you."

When Mrs. Lawson arrived home, she prepared the Sabbath dinner and waited for her husband. The children were anxious to tell their father of the priest's visit to the church. Thirteen-year-old Robert was the first to see his father's car come around the corner. He hurried to the house for the key, and swung the gate open.

"Guess what, daddy," he exclaimed. "That priest was at church today."

"Is it possible?" his father said in amazement. "Let's go in the house. I want to hear more about it."

"Padre Díaz really came to church?" the husband questioned as he greeted his wife.

"Yes, he did," she replied. "It was a thrilling experience for the congregation. I believe this Padre Díaz is in earnest. We talked to him after the service, and he asked me to pray for him. He said he was having a real struggle. Wouldn't it be wonderful if he would accept the Adventist faith?"

"Yes, it would be one of the greatest thrills of our experience. However, he is still a long way off. There are some big hurdles for him."

"Yes, but we must have faith. It may seem as if it isn't possible, but there is nothing too hard for God. After all, it takes a miracle to change anyone's life," Mrs. Lawson said with courage in her voice.

16

THE BITTER CONFLICT

ANDRES returned to his parish with a heavy heart. At the Adventist church, listening to the Bible truth and partaking of Christian fellowship, the way ahead did not look too hard for him. But when he found himself alone, clouds of doubt crowded in upon him. Sometimes he was tempted to wish that he had never heard about the Sabbath and other Bible doctrines that had brought his mind to this confusion.

Every spare moment Andrés spent studying the Bible. The sacredness of the seventh-day Sabbath had been clear to him almost from the beginning, and he realized that he must find a way to keep it. He no longer believed in confession to a priest or in bowing down to saints, although he was forced by circumstances to carry on such services in his church. He modified the order of his services. Candles were used less and less in the church, and he admonished his congregation to study the Bible. The material in *Steps to Christ* was used more and more in his Sunday sermons.

When he considered the subject of man's state in death, he was puzzled. "How can I believe such a materialistic theory? If it weren't for some of these texts in the Bible, I would just forget it."

Over and over again he read the passages he had been

shown. In Ecclesiastes 9:5, 6, he pondered the meaning of the words, "For the living know that they shall die: but the dead know not anything, neither have they any more a reward; for the memory of them is forgotten. Also their love, and their hatred, and their envy, is now perished; neither have they any more a portion forever in anything that is done under the sun."

A few months later, Pastor Lawson was again surprised by a visit from Padre Andrés. "Come in!" the missionary greeted him warmly. "I am so glad to see you."

In the privacy of the pastor's office, Andrés immediately began a discussion of the doctrines he had been studying. "Pastor Lawson, I have read all the books you gave me. I have read and studied many other things on the subject, but I seem unable to accept the doctrine of man's unconsciousness in death."

"I am sure it is not easy to change ideas you have held all your life," the missionary replied. "However, it is not our ideas that count; God's word is the only safe guide. Let's read another text: 'That thou keep this commandment without spot, unrebukable, until the appearing of our Lord Jesus Christ: which in His times He shall show, who is the blessed and only Potentate, the King of kings, and Lord of lords; who only hath immortality, dwelling in the light which no man can approach unto; whom no man hath seen, nor can see: to whom be honor and power everlasting.' 1 Timothy 6:14-16. You see, my friend, the Bible teaches that immortality is a gift that shall be given the righteous at Christ's coming. In 1 Corinthians 15:51-53 we read: 'Behold, I show you a mystery; We shall not all sleep, but we shall all be changed, in a moment, in the twinkling of an eye, at the last trump: for the trumpet shall sound, and the dead shall be raised incorruptible, and we shall be changed. For this corruptible must put on incorruption, and this mortal must put on immortality.' "

For three hours the men discussed this important doctrine. Andrés seemed unwilling to take a plain "Thus saith the Lord." He was argumentative and defensive in his attitude. After what seemed a fruitless discussion, Andrés again left the mission office. Pastor Lawson gave him more books to read, and encouraged him to seek God for guidance and light.

Later that night, in relating the experience to his wife, the missionary said, "I'm afraid the step is too big for him to take. I know that nothing is too hard for God. But, somehow, after today's discussion, I am afraid we won't see him again. Let's continue to pray for him, for the power of God is unlimited."

Andrés went back to his village discouraged and disillusioned. He realized that he had gone to the Adventist pastor to vindicate his own ideas more than to receive help. He had been surprised at the texts the missionary could find to answer his arguments. Could it be that in this, too, he had always been wrong?

Señora Martínez and her husband continued writing to Andrés, encouraging him to study and search for truth. Lengthy discussions took place in letters between the couple and the priest. As the weeks went by, Andrés realized that one by one his former ideas were being replaced by the truth from the Holy Scripture. He was convinced that the Adventists were teaching the Bible truth concerning the soul and man's condition in death. When he was convinced, the rituals, the masses for the dead, and the prayers to the saints became meaningless. Although he now believed the Bible doctrines, he had not made them a part of his life. To change his way of life now, to leave the only thing that was familiar to him, seemed unthinkable. Some days he almost convinced himself that he should forget the upsetting things he had learned and go on in the same old pattern. Would not the Lord accept such a life of sacrifice? Yet when he read his Bible, he knew that he could not go on teaching and practicing things he did not believe.

At this crucial time, Andrés decided to spend ten days in special spiritual exercises and to settle this problem once and for all. He saw no one during this period and ate very little food. He put the Bible and the Adventist literature on one side and the books of doctrine and tradition from his church on the other. Reading first one and then the other, he compared them point by point. While reading the doctrines of the Roman Catholic Church, he felt burdened, perplexed, and unhappy; but when he turned to the Bible and the Adventist literature, the weight lifted from his heart.

At the end of the ten days, Andrés felt constrained to go to a friend, another priest, to make confession.

"You say you have been reading Protestant propaganda?" questioned the white-haired man.

"Yes, padre, I have; but that isn't the worst. I believe it."

"Ah, my son!" continued the old man. "You have made

a great mistake. What prompted you to do such a thing?"

"Well, padre, it is this way," Andrés explained. "For some time I have been concerned over the differences between the doctrines of the church and the Holy Scriptures. My mind has been plagued with doubts for months. Have you never had doubts, padre?"

"Of course, everyone has doubts," said the older man. "But I decided years ago to put such thoughts out of my mind. After all, the mother church is the final authority. I leave such things up to her."

The old priest felt that he had solved the problem for the younger, less experienced man. "After all," the old man had said, "there are some things that can't be explained."

Andrés left his friend, far from satisfied, and thinking, "He may leave his salvation in the hands of the church; but I know I'll have to answer for myself. This is something between me and God. With His help I'll find the answer."

From then on Andrés knew in his heart that he must leave the priesthood; he couldn't live a lie. It was more and more difficult for him to preach with sincerity and to perform the meaningless rites of the church.

"But these people!" he told himself, "all these people in my parish! They have such confidence in me. What will become of them if I leave?"

To run away secretly was unthinkable. "I must pray that God will help me find a way to make this change in my life."

The next big problem facing him was what to do when

he left his parish and renounced the church. He would stand alone without friends or loved ones. He knew that his family would never understand his position. He knew nothing but the priesthood, for he had no training in any form of the practical work of life.

Above the prospect of being without a home or employment was the fact that he had dedicated his life to God. He had served Him to the best of his knowledge all these years, and he had no other desire than to spend the remainder of his life in missionary work. He decided that his only course of action was to place himself in God's hands and expect the Lord to show him the way.

During the time that Andrés served as priest in this coastal community in Guatemala, he had been a friend of Osberto Córdova and his family, with whom he took his meals. Osberto was the only person of the congregation who even suspected that the padre might be sympathetic to the Protestants. Lingering at the table after meals, they enjoyed discussions on many topics. During some of these discussions Andrés had alluded to his reading of the Scriptures. Osberto had faith in the padre's sincerity, and he believed if the priest was examining their church doctrine, he was doing so for some good reason.

One day, after a trip out of town, Andrés was disappointed to learn that he had missed his friend, Pastor Lawson, who had been in the village looking for him.

"Did he say that he would be back?" he asked Señora Córdova.

"No, I think he was on his way to the capital, but he left this note for you," she added, handing it to Andrés.

"I'm sorry to have missed seeing you," the note read. "We have been wondering about you and praying for you." The note added that the missionary would be speaking in a neighboring town that evening.

"How I would love to go to the meeting," Andrés thought; "but I wouldn't dare. I'm too well known in this part of the country."

The tremendous struggle continued in the heart of Andrés. His mind was never at rest, and many times he found himself unable to sleep at night because of his perplexity. Every day he prayed, "Lord, help me find the way. Give me an opportunity. Open a door for me in the impenetrable wall that I face. Most of all, give me the courage and strength to follow Thy leading."

17

A DECISION IS MADE

"**A** LETTER from the superior! Now what can this be about?" Andrés asked himself as he looked through his mail. Tearing open the envelope he read: "You may make plans to take a vacation in Mexico. You will leave for Guatemala City, Wednesday, October 15. In the capital you can arrange your passport and other papers."

This was a surprise for Andrés, for he had received no previous word that a vacation was coming soon. However, the prospect of a few weeks in Mexico was pleasant. One of his mother's sisters lived in Mexico City, and he would enjoy a visit with her.

Andrés made all necessary arrangements for the church services to be conducted properly in his absence, and on the afternoon of October 15, he said good-by to Osberto and boarded the old bus that seemed to be already overflowing with humanity, baggage, and chickens. At the next village Andrés planned to take the night train for Guatemala City. He arrived in good time at the station and was about to buy his ticket, when he saw three familiar faces, one of them his superior. Two other priests were with the stern-faced cleric.

"Padre Andrés, we have been waiting for you," the superior said.

"I am here at your orders," replied Andrés. "I was told

to make preparations for a vacation in Mexico, and that is what I have done."

"We are here to inform you that you are under suspicion of showing sympathy to these Protestant devils and of giving them money."

Andrés's usual good nature vanished and the color came to his face. "It is true that I have donated to people carrying on welfare and missionary work. This is a worthy cause that I can testify to from personal observation after my many years in China. As for their being Protestant devils, I have found nothing about their work or deportment that could possibly class them as devils."

Being in a public place, the superior would not lower his dignity to carry the point further. He said, "Apparently you are already well contaminated by these sons of Luther. You are not leaving for a trip to Mexico, but rather you are being expelled to another country to see if you will repent and forget this heresy. You are to report to the monastery in Guatemala City. There you will arrange your papers and go to Salvador."

While Andrés stood stunned and dumfounded, one of the three priests ordered him to open his suitcase for their inspection, no doubt looking for Protestant propaganda. In this gesture, the zealot was disappointed. He did take out a good suit that Andrés had recently purchased, with the remark, "You won't be needing this."

As Andrés found a seat in the train, he felt his face still burning with the sting of the words and the rough treatment he had received. This was the thanks he received for all his years of service! He had given the best years of his life with never a consideration for his own happiness or comfort. Never in all these years had he received a salary, but only a stipend for his bare necessities. He sat staring out the window, oblivious to everything except his own thoughts. He hardly noticed when the train started, even though there had been the usual bustle of leaving.

As the train rolled through the country, Andrés's thinking began to clear. Could this be the answer to his prayer? He had asked God for the opportunity to follow his convictions. It seemed incredible that it should be brought about in this unexpected turn of events. He had prayed for God to show him the way. Now the answer seemed evident. Was he really going to make this tremendous change in his life?

"If I renounce my faith and my present position, break my connections, and lose all the security I have known, what then? Pastor Lawson has never promised me anything more than the assurance that God will provide a way.

"When I arrive in Guatemala City, I will not go to the monastery," he said to himself. "I will go to the mission office, find Pastor Lawson, and tell him of my decision. I feel sure that he will know what I should do. But what if Pastor Lawson is not there? I know he sometimes goes on trips that take him out of the city for days."

This last thought brought alarm to Andrés. Now that his decision had been made, he must have everything settled soon. "Lord," he prayed, "it may seem like asking a lot; but please let the pastor be there."

Andrés now felt happier than he had for months. His heart was placed in God's hand.

"It matters not what the future holds," he reminded himself. "If I may feel the warmth of His approving smile, I am sure that life will hold nothing too hard for me."

"Well, Padre Andrés! How are you? You must be very happy tonight, singing by yourself." It was one of Padre Andrés's parishioners speaking.

"Pedro, I am glad to see you. Yes, I am happy tonight." Andrés answered his fellow passenger without divulging the thoughts that filled his mind.

As the train, filled with weary passengers, approached the city at dawn, Andrés was troubled by a new thought. "What if they are expecting me at the monastery? What if they have sent someone to meet me at the station?"

It would be better, he decided, to leave the train at the small station at the edge of town and avoid the possibility of further complications. When the train stopped, Andrés and several other passengers got off the train. Andrés hailed the closest taxi and went to a small hotel near the mission office. It was a strange feeling, this new independence!

Andrés was disappointed when he arrived at the office later in the morning, to find that Pastor Lawson was not in. However, he was relieved to know that the president would be in the office that afternoon.

In the afternoon Andrés again came to the mission office. "Good afternoon, señorita, has the pastor arrived yet?" Andrés asked the young lady at the reception desk.

"Oh, yes, Señor Díaz," she smiled. "Pastor Lawson is here, and he is waiting for you." As he followed the secretary to the inner office, Andrés made a mental note:

even the secretaries here radiate a Christian atmosphere.

"Well, what a happy surprise!" Pastor Lawson greeted the priest warmly.

Reassured by the cordial welcome from the missionary, Andrés plunged immediately into the real purpose of his visit. "Pastor Lawson, I have been so anxious to see you. This time I have come to tell you of my decision."

Pastor Lawson listened, studying the expression of the man intently. "What decision have you made, my friend? Tell me about it."

"Pastor, since I saw you several months ago, I have been passing through a crisis. I advanced every possible argument to excuse myself from the obligation of accepting this new doctrine, but it hasn't worked. My mind returned again and again to the same points, and I have finally recognized that it is all founded on the Bible. Today I have come to tell you that if you will believe my sincerity and accept me, I would consider it the highest privilege to be considered a brother of yours in the faith. From this day forth, with God's help, it is my sincere desire and determination to be a Seventh-day Adventist."

For a moment the Adventist pastor was without words to express the thrill and joy that welled up in his heart. He thought, "This is the greatest miracle I ever hope to see." Aloud he said, "Brother Díaz, this is wonderful! Please tell me the whole story."

Andrés recounted his experience, going over the various points of doctrine that had been big hurdles for him. He told of the sleepless nights, the torment of spirit, the hours of doubt and despair, the endless searching and studying, the feeling of an insecure future, and the knowledge of what this decision would mean to his family.

Not having known Andrés personally or his background, the missionary felt it his responsibility to question him thoroughly in regard to his real motives for making this drastic change. There had been cases, he remembered, when deception had been practiced.

However, there was little doubt in Pastor Lawson's mind as to the padre's sincerity or his character, for some of the Adventist members from the district where Andrés had labored had reported their knowledge of the priest, and none of them had intimated anything against his good name. The missionary went over all the main points of doctrine and ascertained that the priest was fully convinced of their soundness.

After a long and intense conversation, Pastor Lawson asked, "And now, Brother Díaz, what are your plans?"

Andrés answered, "I don't have any plans, pastor. As you know, this country is not my home. I came here as a missionary. Now that God has turned me from my former plans and purposes, it seems that I must begin anew. How I am to do that I do not understand as yet."

"I'm sure the future looks very uncertain right now, my friend; but you must have faith that God has a plan for your life," said the missionary. "If you completely dedicate your life and yourself to Him, I am sure that you will find the way He wants you to go. In the meantime, we stand ready to help you. You may count on us as your friends."

Before Andrés left the pastor's office, they knelt for

prayer. Andrés offered a sincere prayer of consecration and submission to God's will, a prayer of thankfulness to God for His Holy Spirit that had guided his life, illumined his mind, and transformed his heart.

After the prayer, the missionary welcomed Andrés into the household of faith with the customary Latin embrace. Each noticed tears brimming in the eyes of his brother. Andrés left the mission office late that afternoon. "God is so good," he said to himself. "I know of a certainty that He has led me. I may not clearly see the future, but with Jesus at my side, I know it will be wonderful."

18

A VISION OF HAPPINESS

PASTOR LAWSON was all smiles as he greeted his family. His wife took him by the coat lapels, saying, "Now, dear, what is the big news? It is written all over your face."

"Andrés, the priest, is here," the missionary said excitedly. "He was in my office all afternoon. He's going to be an Adventist!"

"He's going to be an Adventist!" Mrs. Lawson repeated the words in amazement. Andrés had been mentioned in the family prayers for months; but of late they had almost given up hope, and his name had not been included as often as formerly.

That evening, after the children had been tucked into bed, the minister and his wife sat in front of the glowing embers in the fireplace, discussing the events of the day. The man recounted the long discussion he had had with Andrés. "The problem that confronts him and all of us, is what he shall do next."

"Where is he staying?" questioned Mrs. Lawson.

"At present he is at a little hotel near the office. But he has only about $60, and that won't last long. Do you realize that he never has received a salary? From his fees he took only enough money for his actual expenses, and the rest he turned over to his superiors. I suppose the $60 is money he thought he would need on the trip to Mexico."

"Is he interested in any particular work?"

"No, I don't think so, except to be a missionary. During these years he endeavored to be a missionary for God, and he still has no other desire. Now he longs to preach the advent message."

"God has worked a wonderful miracle in his life. He has brought him to a crisis in his experience, and He must have a plan for his future."

"That is true," continued the pastor. "I believe God has a place for him. We must pray earnestly that we will know how to counsel him wisely."

"Did you tell Andrés that most of our ministers are graduates of our colleges?"

"Yes," her husband answered. "I explained that to him. He has a wonderful spirit. He is ready to sell books or do anything he can. Of course, his real desire is to be a minister; but he realizes that can't come in a day."

The next morning, while the Lawsons were at breakfast, the conversation turned to Andrés, the subject uppermost in the minds of all. "I've been thinking, dear," said the wife. "I believe it would be best to invite Andrés to spend the weekend with us. You know, this will be his first Sabbath. It will be lonesome for him at the hotel. I think he would enjoy sundown worship with us, and Christian friendship on the Sabbath day."

"I think it's a wonderful idea," the husband replied with enthusiasm. "It will mean a lot to Andrés. How will you plan things?"

"There's an extra bed in Robert's room. You wouldn't mind having a roommate, would you, Bob?"

"Me mind? I guess not! It will be something to have a priest for a roommate."

"Of course, he isn't a priest any more, Bob," corrected his father. "I'm sure you two will be good friends."

After morning worship, Pastor Lawson left for the office, and the rest of the family made plans for their guest. Mrs. Lawson arranged the day's work with her two Adventist helpers. Marina, who had been with the family for some time, was indispensable in the cooking, marketing, and laundry work. Elena, a tall, bright-eyed girl, was studying at the business college. She did some work to pay for her room and board.

When the duties had been arranged and everyone was busy, Mrs. Lawson put on a street dress, took her market baskets, and went to make her purchases. Since there were no frozen or canned foods available at prices missionaries can afford, the food for the weekend had to be selected, purchased, and prepared beforehand.

Pastor Lawson found Andrés at the office, waiting for him, when he arrived. "How did everything go with you last night?" the missionary questioned.

"Just fine," Andrés answered, with a broad smile. "I rested the best I have for weeks. It is a tremendous relief to have my mind at peace with God."

"By the way," the pastor continued, "my wife has invited you to spend a few days with us. It will be a pleasure for us if you will come."

"Oh, thank you," Andrés replied and his face brightened. "If it won't be an inconvenience to you and your family, I will consider it a great privilege."

"Then it's settled. I will come by your hotel this afternoon in my car," added the missionary.

Andrés went back to his room to await the hour when Pastor Lawson would call. He had one important task to fulfill. He must write a letter of resignation to his superior. It wouldn't be an easy letter to write; but he was anxious that it reach the authorities before they learned of his whereabouts. He pondered long over the letter, anxious to make it clear that his decision was final. Also he wanted it to be understood that his reasons for leaving the church were doctrinal. At last he was satisfied with the results, and he sealed and mailed the letter. Andrés realized that he had burned his last bridge behind him. There could be no turning back!

Friday afternoon the rambling old house where the Lawsons lived was shining from top to bottom. Robert had cleaned his room, and Elena had polished the mosaic tile floors until they shone. The children, dressed in clean clothes after their baths, were tantalized by the fragrant aromas emanating from the kitchen. There were loaves of freshly baked bread cooling on the shelf in front of the window. Marina was taking the apple pies from the oven, while the last of the soap-scrubbed and disinfected vegetables from the market were ready to go into the refrigerator. As usual, a generous stock of bananas was in the pantry, as well as a basket of avocados. Luscious sweet pineapples and papayas, too, lined the pantry shelves.

"I think everything is finished now, Marina. There's plenty of time before sundown for you to get ready for Sabbath. We'll have soup, homemade bread, stuffed avocados, and a platter of fresh fruit for supper. Pastor Lawson will soon be here with Brother Andrés."

"This will be exciting, señora. Whoever thought I would be getting supper for a priest? Well, anyway, a former priest," Marina added with a chuckle.

"Yes," agreed Mrs. Lawson, "this will be a new experience for all of us."

The sun hung low over the peaks of the towering volcanoes of Guatemala that Friday evening, as Andrés found himself a part of a happy family gathered in the living room. The only light was from the sun's rays as they filtered through the windows and blended with the bright fire on the hearth.

Pastor Lawson began reading: "God is our refuge and strength." The other members of the family joined in repeating the forty-sixth psalm. Afterward they took their Spanish Bibles and read the psalm again in Spanish for the special benefit of Marina and Andrés. Then there was the customary Friday-evening sing, with songs in English and Spanish. Andrés seemed particularly to enjoy this part of the worship hour.

When it was time for prayer, Pastor Lawson explained that it was the custom for each member of the family to offer a short prayer, beginning with Randy and going around the circle.

When it was Andrés's turn, he prayed as one who knew God. "I thank Thee with all my heart, my Saviour, that Thou hast brought me to a knowledge of Thy true Sabbath. On this first Sabbath in my experience, I am happy beyond expression to find myself in Thy flock of believers, and Thou art the Good Shepherd. Accept my life and use it according to Thy divine will."

When worship and supper were over and the children had gone to bed, Andrés sat with Pastor and Mrs. Lawson in the quietness of the Sabbath evening. They reviewed the happenings of recent months, and Andrés recounted more of the struggle he had experienced. They discussed his future and what it might hold for him. When they reluctantly left the dying embers of the fire to go to their rest, Andrés thought, "What could be closer to heaven than a happy Christian home? Tonight I feel the peace, warmth, and security that I have hungered for through the years."

19

AT THE YOUTH CAMP

THE Adventist church members in Guatemala City were surprised to see at the Sabbath school the priest who had visited the service months before, this time without his clerical garb. Andrés enjoyed the Sabbath school immensely. He sat with the Lawson family, and the minister explained the program. The new convert was given a lesson quarterly, and he followed the Bible study with interest. In his mind he constantly compared what he saw with the customs he had always known. He began to understand why all of the Adventists seemed to know their Bibles, for they had them open during Sabbath school, ready to read texts to answer the questions. Then during the church service their Bibles were still open, and the members followed the texts that the minister read.

Before the sermon hour, Pastor Lawson told the congregation some of the experiences the priest had gone through and of his decision to become an Adventist. He then asked Andrés to give his public testimony.

Andrés stood at the pulpit and began: "My esteemed Adventist brothers and sisters: Although this is a reality, it seems almost like a dream to be here with you. Last Sunday, I was a Catholic priest and preached my last sermon in my church on the coast. Today I find myself in an

Adventist church. I have come twice to this church. The first time I came to observe, and I could see the order of the service, the spirit of the members, and the sincere worship. I was convinced by you and your life that this is the true church.

"This, however, was not enough for my conversion. It is difficult to change the thinking of one who has studied for thirteen years in theology, philosophy, and the sciences; but human intelligence must humble itself before the divine word. My mind was not easily convinced; it was a struggle. Human science cannot compare with divine science. God can help the most humble to withstand the strongest attacks.

"My brothers and sisters, God has done a marvelous work for me. As some of you may know, a Señora Martínez first began to talk to me about the Bible. I was astounded at how much she knew of the Holy Scriptures. She talked of many doctrines; some I accepted, and some I refused.

"After she had gone, the words she had spoken concerning the Sabbath remained in my heart. I was steeped in the traditions of the church, for since my childhood I had known nothing else. There were some things that I could not harmonize with the Bible. I don't mean to say that the Catholic Church has no good in it. But I had been convinced that there was no salvation outside of the Catholic Church and that the pope was infallible. Yet certain rites of the church had always puzzled me.

"The study of the Bible and the prayers of God's people have helped me greatly. An Adventist brother took pains to explain point by point the Adventist doctrines, but when he came to the state of the dead, I could not believe that death is a sleep. Brother Martínez wrote letters to me, explaining this Adventist doctrine in relation to the Catholic teachings and traditions. It was not easy, I assure you, to change from the Catholic doctrine to the Adventist teachings.

"I can say sincerely that conversion is a work of God. Faith is not the result of science or culture; it comes to the soul that humbles itself before the word of God. I am like Paul in that I persecuted the Protestants. I repeat the words of Paul that, having persecuted the Christians and having given sermons against them, today I want to be a disciple. Although I should be the last to enter heaven, to me the important thing is someday to enter and sit down among the sons of God.

"Three days ago when I was coming by train to the city, I felt very sad. I had a great desire to see Pastor Lawson. I was afraid he might be out. But finally I found him, thanks to God. I presented my case with its seemingly insurmountable mountains of obstacles. Finally, with his help, I decided to be one of your brothers. We prayed together and gave each other a fraternal embrace.

"I am happy to be here with you. I will be happy even if I have the lowest place in the kingdom of heaven. I give thanks to God that He showed me the light and that I may enter through the gates of heaven."

When Andrés sat down, there was scarcely a dry eye in the crowded room. It was a day of great rejoicing for the members of the church, a time of reconsecration and rededication by them to the precious advent message.

Later Pastor Lawson said to Andrés, "Ever since your last visit here, these people have been praying for you. Today they have seen the answer to their prayers, and their hearts are full of joy."

Sunday morning all was bustling at the Lawson household, for this was the opening day of the youth camp for Adventist young people of Guatemala. They would be gathering from the highlands, the coast, and the villages in between. Robert had been looking forward to this meeting that was to be held at a rural boarding school belonging to the government. During vacation time this camp beside a mountain creek, nestled in tall pines, was available for Adventist youth.

"Do you have everything packed, Robert?" mother asked from the doorway of his room. "Have you checked the list we made out?"

"Yes, mom, I think I have everything. Which blankets do you want me to take?"

"Let's see," answered his mother, as she looked through the stack of bedding. "Daddy and Andrés will be staying there part of the time, too, so we'll have to be sure there's plenty of bedding for everyone. Here are the sheets and a quilt, and the two warm blankets. They should be enough."

"Thanks, mom. I think I'm ready now. We're to leave by one o'clock."

After a quick dinner, the three campers loaded the car and met the group of young people at the chartered bus. Robert rode on the bus; Andrés and Pastor Lawson would drive out later with a load of supplies for the kitchen.

The details of the camp had been well planned, and when the group arrived, each young person was assigned to a unit with a counselor. The dormitories were arranged around a spacious cement patio, the girls' building on one side and the boys' on the other. The dormitories were in barracks style, with the beds lined up in large rooms. Soon the beds were made and the suitcases put away, and the campers were ready for activity.

Andrés marveled at the camp when he arrived. Suppertime found an enthusiastic group of sixty-five young people filing into the dining hall. They ate with their own units, and after the meal they washed their own dishes in tubs of sudsy water and rinsed them in pots of boiling water suspended over a bonfire.

Andrés went on hikes with the young people. He listened with interest to their testimonies during the devotional periods and laughed with them when they let off their energy at the swimming pool. Through it all he was impressed over and over with the clean, courteous Christian youth.

On Sabbath morning the campers gathered for Sabbath school in the "Cathedral of the Pines." Many parents and friends of the young people came to spend the day with them. It was thrilling to hear the congregation sing, and the melodies carried through the woods. Pastor Lawson spoke during the worship hour, and he made a special appeal for the young people to dedicate their lives to God. It was an hour long to be remembered. Andrés felt a thrill of happiness as he realized that he was one of these people.

He saw genuine religion at work changing and directing the lives of young people.

When most of the campers gathered in the dining room for the noon meal, Mrs. Lawson, Marina, and Elena quickly spread their food on one of the unused tables. "Mommie, may we go with the campers on their nature walk this afternoon?" pleaded Jeanie and Margaret. "They won't tell us where we are going; we have to wait and see. On this walk no one is supposed to talk. May we go?"

Mrs. Lawson laughed and said, "It sounds very mysterious. Yes, girls, you may go, if you promise to stay in line and do what you are told."

"Oh, goody!" they both shouted, as they left on a run.

Andrés joined the young people on the nature walk. He enjoyed the entire afternoon immensely, feeling that this meeting on the mountainside was a fitting climax to the Sabbath day, his second Sabbath since he had joined the commandment-keeping people.

20

GROWING IN FAITH

"DADDY, there's a man at the gate. Shall I let him in?" Robert called to his father one Sunday afternoon. It was one of those rare occasions when all the family were at home together.

"Just a minute, Bob, I'll go. I have the key right here," his father replied.

A short time earlier the missionary and his wife had been suspicious of a man who came to the gate on the pretext of looking for someone. He returned three different times. He came again at three o'clock in the morning with a gun and attempted to get through the high iron gate. Since that time the children and maids had been given instructions not to open the gate when strangers appeared.

"Good afternoon, señor. I am looking for the Padre Andrés Díaz. Is he here?" said the man as Pastor Lawson came to the gate.

"Yes, he is here. I don't believe I have the pleasure of knowing you." Pastor Lawson thought it best to inquire who the visitor was, and to be certain that Andrés wanted to see him, before he opened the gate.

"I am Osberto Córdova. I am Padre Andrés's friend."

When one of the children told Andrés of his visitor, he sent word back that he was anxious to talk to his friend.

As Señor Córdova was ushered into the house, Andrés came forward and gave him a cordial welcome. The two men were given the privacy of the living room. However, Mr. Córdova surprised them by saying, "Please, will you join us? What I have to say is for you to hear, too."

As they seated themselves at one end of the large living room, Andrés explained to the Lawsons that Mr. Córdova was the proprietor of a business in the town where he had served as priest. He also added that Osberto was the president of the church committee.

Osberto began, "You folks, no doubt, wonder why I have come. You may think that I have been sent here to persuade Padre Andrés to come back, but that is not the case. On the contrary, I have come to commend him into your hands. He has been a good padre and served our community unstintingly. We hope that you will love him as we have."

It was obvious to Pastor and Mrs. Lawson that Andrés was deeply touched. They understood a little of what it had cost him to leave the flock he had raised up.

Pastor Lawson answered, "Thank you, Mr. Córdova; we are glad you have come. You may be assured that we are more than interested in our brother's welfare. It has taken great courage, but God has led him and He will not forsake him."

Osberto then revealed that he, too, had been reading and studying Adventist literature. "I am not sure but that it may be right," he confessed. "In fact, I have already begun to keep the seventh-day Sabbath. If only Padre Andrés could come back to our village and teach us the

Bible doctrines, I am sure that many of the people would listen."

The missionary and his wife exchanged knowing glances, each thinking of the experience of a former priest who had been accepted into one of the Protestant churches. In a village not far from their home this priest began preaching his new beliefs; but an angry mob forced its way into the meeting and killed the man with machetes before the horrified audience. Elder and Mrs. Lawson knew that Andrés was in danger from prejudiced and fanatical people.

"It may be that an evangelist can be sent to your village, Señor Córdova," the missionary explained. "Just now, it seems best for Brother Andrés to study a little longer."

Andrés inquired of his friend concerning his personal belongings that he had left behind. To the surprise of the Lawsons and Andrés, Osberto replied, "Well, padre, after you left that day, I had a premonition that something out of the ordinary was happening. I went to your room that afternoon, put all of your belongings in your trunk, and had it moved to my house. The next morning three priests came to my door. They wanted to know where your things were. When I asked them what they wanted with them, they said they wanted to send them to you. I told them that I would take care of that. They were very insistent and almost abusive. I didn't give them anything or tell them where your things were. I asked them why they had treated you in such a deceitful way. I wanted to know why you had been taken away without having an opportunity to tell the people good-by. For this they had no

answer. I went so far as to ask them if they pretended to
be ministers of God, and they said that they were. I told
them that ministers of God would not lie as they had done.
We feel very sad in our village over this episode. Personally, my faith in the church has been shaken. I hardly
know what to think or believe."

Pastor Lawson assured Osberto that man cannot put
faith in other people. "We must study truth for ourselves
from God's word, and then follow Jesus."

Before leaving, Osberto said, "If any attempt should be
made to defame Padre Andrés or cast reflection on his life,
we who are of his former parish will defend his character
in the newspaper with a thousand signatures."

"Thank you, Señor Córdova," Pastor Lawson said. "We
are grateful for your visit. I am sure it has been cheering
to Brother Andrés. We are happy to have made your
acquaintance. Please consider us your friends and come to
our house whenever you are in the city."

Then, after making arrangements to send Andrés his
trunk containing his belongings, Osberto left.

Pastor Lawson discussed the turn of events with
Andrés. "After Mr. Córdova's account of the priests
who came after your belongings, I feel somewhat concerned. You know their way of dealing and thinking better than we do. What do you think, Andrés? How far do
you think they might go?"

Andrés pondered the question. "Of course, what I have
done is a grave offense to them. I suppose I might disap-
pear if they had their way. I know I wouldn't want to be
under their power right now."

"I believe, Andrés, that it would be well to take all possible precautions, especially when you are on the street alone," cautioned the American.

In later days Andrés sometimes accompanied Pastor Lawson to the mission office, where he studied and read. On one occasion, Andrés and the pastor drove up to the mission office just as another man arrived. He wore clerical garb, and Andrés recognized him as the superior of his order from another Central American country. The missionary went on into his office and left Andrés to visit in the patio with the priest.

"Who is that man you came in with?" questioned the superior.

"Oh, that is my friend, Pastor Lawson," replied Andrés.

"No, I mean, who is he? What does he do?" persisted the superior.

"Well," Andrés began to explain again, "he is the president of the mission here. He is in charge of all the churches in Guatemala."

"But what is his title?" pressed the older priest.

Finally Andrés answered in a way that seemed to satisfy the priest. "I guess you might say that he is the archbishop."

The visiting priest launched into the reason for his visit. "I have come, Padre Andrés, to help you to see the folly of the course you have taken. When I received word that you had renounced your holy vows, and had even renounced your faith, I was shocked beyond words. I couldn't believe it. So I decided to come and see for myself. I am sure there has been some misunderstanding."

Andrés replied quickly, "There was a misunderstanding, all right, a misunderstanding that possibly hastened my decision."

Andrés recounted the undignified and unfair way that he had been treated at the railroad station by the three priests.

"Don't let that experience affect you too much," the priest added, attempting to smooth the matter over. "The superior who handled the affair has been severely censured. In fact, he has been moved, and you will not have to deal with him any more. We want you to come back. We will welcome you with open arms."

"No, I'm afraid that is impossible," Andrés replied thoughtfully. "Actually, the bitter experience of being sent away from the parish that I loved was not the real reason for my leaving the church. I left because I no longer believe the things that the church teaches. Being expelled from Guatemala only provided the experience that I had been praying for—a way to change my life. There is no turning back for me. I have experienced such great joy in following the simple teachings of Jesus that the past seems dark."

"Padre Andrés, you must reconsider. You know as well as I that there is only one church, and that there is no salvation outside the church. You have been terribly deceived." The superior was earnest in his appeal.

"No," spoke Andrés with conviction, "I am not deceived. I wasted many years of my life believing things that are not true. When I discovered that the teachings of the church and the teachings of the Bible were not in harmony, I decided that I must take my stand for the Bible and the Bible only."

"Your pride has been hurt, padre," the older man persisted. "You mustn't make a decision so quickly. If you will come back, the whole affair will be forgotten. You can even have your choice of your future work. I plead with you, reconsider."

Andrés was not tempted to return. He felt, however, that the interest and affection of his former superior was sincere. In his heart he longed to share his new faith with this man. He ventured to try. "Padre, my decision is final. However, I would like for you to understand some of the reasons for this change in my life. Have you never noticed the inconsistencies in the doctrines of the church as compared with the Bible?"

"I don't worry over those," the priest said with a shrug of his shoulders. "The church is the final authority, the pope is infallible, and, furthermore, the Bible was written only for the learned doctors and scholars to interpret. If you are not willing to listen to reason, I must go."

When he was alone again, Andrés reviewed his conversation with the superior. He was saddened as he thought of the spiritual darkness that clouded the minds of his former co-workers. Somehow a ray of light had pierced through the darkness to his own mind, and gradually the darkness had been dispelled. He longed to tell the things that were in his heart, to help others see how simple it is to follow Jesus Christ. He determined to dedicate the rest of his life in giving the good news of the Bible to those in darkness.

Andrés received many letters, primarily from other priests. Some denounced him, some pleaded with him to come back. One letter in particular touched the former priest, because it came from a dear friend. The missive expressed the sorrow of the friend because of the step Andrés had taken. Andrés longed to show his friend the plain truth of God's word. He answered the letter in these words:

"MY VERY ESTEEMED FRIEND:

"I received your affectionate letter, which I read with much interest. I thank you sincerely for the sentiments manifested toward me. In your letter you showed grave concern over my decision to begin a new way in the Christian life. I must tell you sincerely that I find myself very happy being an Adventist. This is not just another Protestant religion invented by Luther. It did not arise in the sixteenth century, and it is not a sect invented by human philosophy.

"The Adventist religion is based on truth God gave to the patriarchs and prophets in the Old Testament. It rests on the teachings of the Son of God, Jesus Christ, who by His words and example during the three years of His missionary life gave the words of life to men, words without a shadow of error. On the Day of Pentecost the apostles understood the complete doctrine of their divine Master. The sum of this apostolic preaching is to know Christ by faith; to give testimony of this faith with good works; to keep the mind from all error, superstition, idolatry; to know Christ as the only Mediator; to claim redemption from eternal perdition by His blood on Calvary; to allow Him to cleanse our hearts from all sin and prepare us for His second coming and the resurrection.

"This is the Adventist religion that has been kept pure and without adulteration. The Ten Commandments are observed without change or modification.

"Among the congregations of the faithful Adventists, the term 'brother' is used as was customary among the early apostles. The same charity reigns among them in spiritual or economic matters. Vice and sin are energetically kept out of the church. There is love of God, and an understanding of His mercy and His abhorrence of evil. There is a strict vigilance to uphold religious principles by careful and constant study of the Sacred Scriptures. Altogether, there is a perfume of pure Bible teaching without the adulteration by human rites.

"Because of all this, I feel very happy to belong to the small flock that with all faithfulness keeps and conserves the transcendent Decalogue of Sinai.

"Sincerely your friend,

"ANDRES."

One Sunday afternoon when Andrés was joining a social hour with the young people in the patio of the mission office, the friend who had written to the former priest came looking for him. He had come to remonstrate with Andrés and rescue him from Protestant heresy. On this occasion Pastor Lawson invited the two men to use his private office for conversation.

As the men discussed doctrines and theology, one of the Adventist young men had to go to a small storeroom next to the president's office. He was able to hear the conversation clearly. He reported to the mission president: "Pastor Lawson, Brother Andrés is quoting text after text, and the poor fellow can't answer him. Brother Andrés told him that any of the Adventist children of ten or twelve years of age could put him to the wall when it comes to knowing the Bible."

Since this particular priest had been his special friend, Andrés tried to help him to see that in the judgment he must answer to God for his beliefs. There could be no hiding behind the teachings of any church or any man. He begged his friend to study the Bible for himself and to have the courage to follow its teachings.

"No," answered his visitor, "I'll have to take my chances as I am now, for my life is too firmly planted and grounded. Even though I might doubt, I could never change."

"Pastor Lawson," Andrés said one evening as they lingered at the supper table in conversation, "when can I be baptized? I am anxious to be a member of God's remnant church."

"I am glad to hear you say that," answered the missionary. "To be baptized, a person simply gives his heart to God, understands and believes the doctrines, and is willing to make Jesus the center of his life. We have gone over the beliefs and practices of the church, but we will systematically go through them again. Perhaps there may be some things you would like to study more fully."

After several days of special Bible studies and many more hours of private study, Andrés was ready to be baptized. There were four others in the baptismal class of the church, who were waiting for the next baptismal service. Among these was Robert, Pastor Lawson's son. A Sabbath was set for the special service, and Andrés looked forward to it as a significant moment in his life.

At the appointed hour, the church was filled. For Pastor and Mrs. Lawson, it was a high day in their lives. After the mission president had given a short talk on baptism and the responsibilities of church membership, the candidates were called to the front of the church.

The last two candidates were Robert and Andrés. As the former priest presented himself for baptism, he thought back over the struggles and discouragement he had faced. It seemed that he was stepping from one world into another. Although the future was uncertain, yet his faith was growing every day. He felt a serenity in his soul as he followed in the footsteps of his Master.

According to their custom, the church members formed a line and followed the church officers in giving a personal welcome to each newly baptized member. Andrés's heart was warmed as these brothers and sisters in the faith welcomed him with Christian love. The service ended as all joined in singing the hymn, "Blest be the tie that binds."

The only cloud on the horizon for Andrés was the thought of his mother and brother in Spain who knew nothing of his new faith and the change in his life. He must find a way to bring them the message of truth.

Since the Lawson family had spent five years in Guatemala, it was time for them to go to America on their furlough. Arrangements were made for Andrés to accompany them as far as Mexico City. From there he would go to the Adventist college at Montemorelos and wait for his papers to enter the United States. It was his ambition to prepare to serve in the Adventist Church.

"It doesn't seem possible that this is our last night in Guatemala, does it?" Mrs. Lawson said to her husband as they roamed through the now empty rooms of the big house among the trees.

"It gives one a lonesome feeling to think of leaving," replied the pastor.

The Lawsons and Andrés had moved to a small hotel for this last night. Final arrangements for leaving had been made and the last suitcase packed. At about two o'clock in the morning Marina and Mrs. Lawson finished cleaning the empty house. Pastor Lawson took Marina to the home of friends, left his wife at the hotel, where the children were sleeping, and with dragging steps went to the office to complete the last details. About four in the morning he crawled into a hard but welcome bed at the hotel.

The plane left at seven thirty in the morning. Saying good-by is never a pleasant experience, but when missionaries leave a field where they have lived and worked for a number of years, the strong ties are hard to break. The lobby of the airport was filled with many church members who had come to bid the Lawsons farewell.

Andrés, too, felt a twinge in his heart as he was leaving these people who had welcomed him into their midst with open arms. There were many embraces and farewell words. However, clocks do not wait for important moments, and all too soon the call came over the loud-speaker, "The plane is now loading."

The departing group pulled themselves away and boarded the plane. The friends on the airport terrace could still be seen waving their last good-bys as the plane rose from the runway and headed north.

At Mexico City the time had come for Andrés to bid the Lawson family farewell. The ties between them had become strong, and it was with sadness and reluctance that they parted.

"Don't worry, Andrés," said Pastor Lawson. "Everything will work out for the best. You will soon have your papers arranged and be on your way to the United States. We will be looking forward to seeing you."

"I know, pastor; and my faith is strong. It is just that I have come to love you and your family as if you were my own," Andrés said.

"We feel the same about you, Andrés," Mrs. Lawson added. "Don't let anything discourage you, for the Lord has something good in store for your life."

21

A GLORIOUS DAY!

"**L**OOK, mamma, what I found!" Small Pedrito handed his mother a handbill that he had picked up from their porch.

"Will Communism Rule the World?" Señora Vásquez read on the attractive handbill her son gave her. She read on through the folder, but at the bottom of the sheet she saw something that caused her eyes to grow big in surprise. "Former priest, Padre Andrés Díaz, will speak each evening."

The señora showed the handbill to the other members of her family, genial Pancho, her husband, and the three teen-age children. "Let's go and hear him," she said. "If he has been a priest, then it should be all right to listen to what he has to say."

The following Sunday evening found the Vásquez family in the hall with many other Spanish-speaking people.

Andrés had been called by the Seventh-day Adventist denomination to do evangelistic work for Spanish-speaking people in a Midwestern conference. During the last few months Andrés had been associated with Pastor Castillo, and the pastor's family had been a great help to the new worker in the district. Night after night the hall was filled with interested listeners. The Vásquez family was there almost every night. Andrés, untiring in his efforts, spent the morning studying diligently and preparing sermons. In the afternoon he visited in the homes of the people, going over the points of doctrine that they did not understand, and encouraging them to keep searching for truth.

Andrés rented a modest room and took his meals with a family in the neighborhood. He was happy and content in his busy life for God. He received letters regularly from the Lawson family, whose interest and encouragement never ceased.

When the meetings ended, Pastor Castillo conducted the baptismal service. Andrés felt a thrill of joy as each one was lowered into the water.

"Pastor Castillo, what shall we do about a permanent church home for these new believers?" Andrés asked after the baptism. "The hall where they are meeting isn't a suitable place for Sabbath services."

"That is true, Andrés. We need a church. Let me consult the conference president; we will see what can be done."

On Sabbaths a group from the nearby English church continued coming to help Andrés in the service. Among those who came was a young woman, Carol Andrews, who had taken a special interest in the children's department. There were always plenty of children in the thriving Sabbath school. During the church services she played the piano.

One Sabbath Carol's mother said to Andrés, "Brother Díaz, we have a girl named Angela working in our home who speaks only a little English. I have been wondering if you would visit her. It is possible she would be interested in studying the message."

"Of course I will be glad to visit Angela. When would be a convenient time to call?"

"Well, she is there most of the time," the woman replied. "Come whenever it is convenient."

Andrés visited Angela and found her interested in studying the Bible. He helped her enroll in the Voice of Prophecy correspondence lessons.

After considering the need, the conference committee gave Andrés permission to go forward with plans and money-raising for a suitable church building. With the co-operation of all the members the building soon was in the process of construction. The day came when the church was ready for the dedication service. The members and their families were present, and in addition there were interested friends. It was a thrilling hour for Andrés!

The young evangelist was lonely, however, and this feeling was accentuated when he went to workers' meeting or social gatherings, or visited members in their homes. He wondered if he could find a Christian girl to be his companion, one who would stand by him in his ministry. On Sabbath he would glance in the direction of Carol Andrews at the piano.

Now the girl sat in the first pew behind the piano, her eyes fixed upon the speaker. She was an attractive blonde, slim and not too tall. While her physical attributes appealed to him, it was something more in Carol that he admired. She was a sincere Christian. Her greatest interest was in the church, and her dress and deportment were appropriate for an Adventist girl. She was also a graduate nurse, who had dedicated her training to humanity.

"Actually," Andrés thought to himself, "I have no reason to hope for Carol. She has never given me any reason. But—well, it seems that she would be an ideal minister's wife."

The next time he went to visit at the Andrews home, Andrés arrived at a time when he thought Carol might not be on duty at the hospital. He was not disappointed. After studying with Angela, Andrés tried to engage Carol in conversation; but his English lacked polish and he was painfully inadequate in social graces with young women.

Carol sensed his discomfort and she did what she could to ease the situation. Before leaving he gathered courage to ask, "Would you consider going to the district meeting with me next Sabbath?"

Andrés had purchased a car of not-too-recent model soon after entering the United States.

"Well, yes, Brother Díaz, I would enjoy going with you. Thank you," Carol replied.

"If you don't mind, Carol, just call me Andrés. 'Brother Díaz' sounds so formal."

Carol smiled. "Fine then, Andrés."

When Andrés arrived at Carol's door on Sabbath morning, he said to himself, "I wonder what in the world is the matter with me. I never felt so nervous and frightened in my life!"

Mrs. Andrews invited the young minister in, and Carol soon stood in the doorway ready to go. As he looked at her he thought, "She is even prettier than I remembered, especially her smile." Carol did have a beautiful smile, which displayed perfect teeth. Her expression always seemed pleasant, and, knowing her, one could hardly think of her as ever having a bad disposition even for a moment.

The day went by all too fast for Andrés. He had endured so many years of loneliness—everywhere alone. Sitting beside Carol in the meetings, he knew that this was the way he would build a new life, if she would consent.

As days and weeks went by, the friendship between Andrés and Carol grew. The man now had a real incentive to work diligently on his English. One evening, when Andrés brought Carol home from a party, he said, "Carol, I know I am not worthy to ask you, but I love you and I wish you would be my wife. I don't have much to offer, but I need your sweetness and Christian influence and love. We both trust in God and are devoted to His work. I think we could be happy together."

Carol did not answer at first. She looked straight ahead, her face serious. Then with a faint smile she turned in Andrés's direction and answered, "You have come to mean a great deal to me, Andrés. It is a serious responsibility to be a minister's wife. Marriage is such a solemn thing and of so much importance, I would like a little time to consider it and pray about it. I must be sure it is God's will."

"It will be as you say, Carol. I will wait, but not too patiently, for your decision. I have been praying, and I will continue to pray that God will direct us. When may I come back for your answer?"

"Let's make it a week from tonight, Andrés."

The ensuing week dragged by for the man, and it was

hard for him to concentrate on his work. What would he do if her answer was No?

When the excited and frightened Andrés finally found himself at Carol's home, the girl opened the door and invited him in. The living room was empty, but there was the sound of dishes rattling in the kitchen where Angela was working.

Carol and Andrés sat on the sofa in an awkward silence. Finally the young man said abruptly, "Carol, this has been a long week. Tell me, please, what your answer is."

"The answer is Yes," Carol said simply.

There were plans to be laid. Andrés was anxious for the wedding to be as soon as possible. Carol did not want a large wedding, so they planned a quiet, simple ceremony in the home of their mutual friends, the Castillo family.

Pastor Castillo stood in front of a bank of flowers in the living room, and Carol and Andrés faced him. With many church members and relatives to witness the ceremony, the couple pledged their troth and received the blessing of heaven. Andrés felt that his world of the past —the days of youth and of the priesthood—were fading into the mist of memory. He had roamed over the world, but in the end God had worked things out for his good and his happiness. The path ahead seemed straight and bright. Hand in hand, he and Carol would face the future, knowing that the Master was leading them. God had brought him out of darkness and given him a place in His work and a Christian helpmeet to stand by his side. Truly he was "a firebrand plucked out of the burning."